FABULOUS FRENCH FRU

A harvest of recipes from the fields, woodlands and orchards of the world – all interpreted with that special French flair!

FABULOUS FRENCH FRUIT CUISINE

Gourmet French Fruit Recipes
From a Master Chef

Jean Conil and Fay Franklin

THORSONS PUBLISHING GROUP

First published 1988

© JEAN CONIL and FAY FRANKLIN 1988

Illustrated by Angela Barnes

Colour photography and styling
by Sue Atkinson, Mike Roles Studios

British Library Cataloguing in Publication Data

Conil, Jean
Fabulous French fruit cuisine: gourmet
recipes.
1. Cookery (Fruit)   2. Cookery, French
I. Title II. Franklin, Fay
641.6'4   TX811

ISBN 0-7225-1277-5

Published by Thorsons Publishers Limited, Wellingborough,
Northamptonshire, NN8 2RQ, England.

Typeset by BookEns, Saffron Walden, Essex
Printed in Great Britain by The Bath Press, Bath, Avon

1   3   5   7   9   10   8   6   4   2

Contents

Introduction

'Give me books, fruit, French wine and fine weather and a little music out of doors,
played by somebody I do not know.'

– John Keats

The 'new wave' of French cuisine that typified the late 1970s and early 80s has now subdued into a way of eating that is as healthy as the more spartan excesses of nouvelle cuisine and as satisfying as the feasts of the classical days that preceded it. While chefs are understandably reluctant to give up the chance to create food that is beautiful to behold, they have now put aside the studied minimalism of the single perfect tomato rose and arrangements of two mangetout peas and a single baby carrot in favour of a freshness of colour, flavour and style. This could not have come about without the nouvelle revolution, and the progress now being made by young cooks, from California to Chelsea, Paris to Perth, is one which I welcome heartily.

One of the benefits that has remained with us in the new style of cooking from the upheaval in the kitchens of the past decade, is the use of fruits in a wide range of dishes. Yet this technique is, in fact, one which harks back to ancient times. The Romans and Greeks scented their food with fragrant flowers and fruits, sweetening their meat dishes in a way that, today, we would find cloying and unappealing. The traditions of our ancestors have gradually subsided during the past century, and until recently fruit sauces with savoury dishes were confined to the mandatory apple sauce with pork, cranberry with turkey, and so forth.

It is, perhaps, the influence of the cuisines of far-flung lands, now coming to be part of everyone's widening eating habits, that has helped to bring back fruit into the mainstream of cooking – India and the Orient have been especially influential in their imaginative mixing of sweet and savoury ingredients to form a balanced and delicious whole. And it is the growing vegetarian and demi-veg following, I feel, that has served to take these influences and make the most of them in Western cuisine. It is, of course, especially for them that this book was devised, although I sincerely hope that it will be welcomed by inventive and imaginative cooks of all persuasions.

The other revolution that has taken place in all our homes in the past few years is the tremendous awareness that has developed about the quality of the food we eat. No longer are we content to simply remove from our supermarket shelves the cans, packets and anonymous film-wrapped parcels that the manufacturers had, for so long, been turning out as part of the convenience food boom. At last, we began to realize that convenience was taking priority over a far more important concern – that of our health, and the health of our children (and thus the health of the future). To be fair, the food producers have caught on quickly to the mood of the consumer, for only by giving the public what it demands could the manufacturers and suppliers hope to survive the onslaught of these new demands. So we have had a barrage of additive-free-this, low-fat-that, and high-fibre-other. Freshness has become a prized commodity in our markets.

Freshness is an integral part of a diet that espouses a strong emphasis on fruit and vegetables, seeds and grains, and dairy produce (albeit in lesser amounts). In eating such a diet we must, of course, be aware of the perils of a whole new range of additives – and they are those which, worryingly, appear on no label with an E-number for you to identify. These additives are the pesticide residues, left from crop spraying that is a part of today's intensive farming and the seeming need of the consumer for perfectly-formed, uniformly-sized, clean vegetables. They are the chemicals drawn up by the plants from soil enriched by chemical fertilizers, to give us bright green lettuces in the middle of Winter, fat red strawberries in May. And they are the preservatives that coat the peel of our citrus fruit to give them a longer shelf life . . . what is the poor consumer to do? Is our seemingly healthy diet actually any more good for us than the colourings and flavourings we have so recently dismissed from our kitchen cupboards? Well, yes it is, if you choose carefully and make as much noise about these outrages as you did about those other problems!

Some enterprising retailers are now giving shelf space to organic produce. At the time of writing, you will probably have to pay a little extra for, say, an organic apple than its commercially-produced counterpart. And it may have the odd speckle and shading to its skin, and you may have to pick and choose if you badly need four of exactly the same size. No, it won't necessarily be a silken-smooth, spherical bright green orb – but it will have real taste, just like the apples you recall from childhood, rather than tasting like sweet, soft cotton wool. And, more importantly, it will not be doing you any harm. Surely those few pennies extra are worth paying, especially if it is in the knowledge that the more you buy, the more will be produced, and thus prices will soon come down. Exciting, too, is the way that the smaller, organic producer is turning to a wider variety of each fruit, going back to traditional favourites rather than concentrating on just the high-cropping strains.

Exotic fruit is another option appearing with increasing frequency on our market stalls and shelves. Choose your supplier with care, of course, in the light of what has just been said, but the key to the new availability of such produce is the refrigerated air cargoes. These supply us with fruit grown in regions where intensive farming techniques are not as over-exploited as they have been in more developed parts of the world, and so such fruit is usually a fresh, healthy purchase.

Fresh and healthy. Isn't that the very essence of fruit's appeal? In its various forms it brings us vitamin C, as every child knows, fibre, iron, calcium and that healthier, more slowly absorbed form of sugar called fructose. It improves our appetite and our digestion. It brings variety to our diet. Fresh or dried, it is a healthy and satisfying snack that is relatively low in calories – as long as you don't succumb to the easy temptation of over-indulging in some of the dried varieties! It forms a large part of our diet, and yet we use it in such unimaginative ways. There is nothing wrong with that, to be sure – better to eat fruit plain and simple than not at all, and certainly better than to stew it until all its goodness has gone. However, I hope you will find, in the pages that follow, a new sense of inspiration, to accompany you when you next visit the fruit stall or the supermarket display.

You will find all sorts of unexpected uses for fruit, whether common or exotic. Soups, salads, casseroles, fricassees and savoury bakes, as well as the more familiar fruited cakes, pies, desserts and sauces. At the end of the book, by way of a light-hearted finish, you will discover a whole section of drinks recipes, both alcoholic and teetotal. Whichever you choose will bring an air of luxury to your table or your party, and many (though not all) cost very little to create. You will find fruit of every variety, from the humble, splendid apple to the strange new fruits you may have seen and wondered how to use. You will find recipes to help you use up an Autumn glut, and those which will give you the opportunity to shop and experiment especially; recipes to whip up for a quick lunch, supper or breakfast, and those to serve for a special occasion; recipes for health and those for sheer hedonism.

The versatility of fruit allows all these opposites to sit happily, shoulder to shoulder, within these pages – what a delight, to have at our disposal the greatest cornucopia of all!

Happy cooking!

CHAPTER ONE

Les Potages aux Fruits en Compote

Soups from the Orchard

A fruit soup is still considered to be quite a coup in the modern restaurant – there is such a strong link in the minds of most diners that fruit is for dessert, because it is sweet, that the chef serving a bowl of chilled cherry soup, for example, may well find he has plenty left at the end of the evening.

Yet what could be more refreshing? How better to begin a gourmet dinner than with a delicate bowl of fruit soup, that serves to whet the appetite without sating it, that balances sharp and sweet, that captivates the tastebuds without overwhelming them before the meal is truly underway? Chefs are growing in awareness of the versatility of fruit-based soups – now it is up to the adventurous customer to give them a try.

Why not experiment with this delightful style of cooking at home first? When Summer brings gluts of wonderful produce to garden and market, it is a pleasure indeed to be able to create pans of subtle and exquisite soup – to eat now, or to freeze for the future.

If you are really unsure of the appeal of a fruit soup, why not try one of the more substantial soups in this chapter as a breakfast? For those who cannot stomach a hearty breakfast, this is a perfect way to restore flagging energy levels, wake up the system and take in a good balance of essential nutrients.

The beautiful Franche-Comté region of France has a bounty of orchard produce in its green fields, that lie in valleys or on plateaux amongst the dramatic Jura mountains. It is a region with a character all its own, despite lying between several more well-known neighbours – Alsace lies to the North, Champagne and Burgundy to the East, the Rhône Valley to the South, and Switzerland to the West. Its wines are connoisseur's items, especially the rich and heady *Vin Jaune*, the yellow wine found only here, and the magical *Vin Fou*, the 'mad wine' of Arbois, with its sparkle and character. The fruit of the region is primarily the cherry, and in Spring parts of this region are white with blossom. The Haute-Saône is renowned for its Eaux de Vie, liqueurs that beat even

Kirsch in the esteem of the gourmet. But cherry is not the only flavour – plums, raspberries and many other fruits can be used to equally splendid advantage.

But it is the cherry that provides the traditional Franche-Comté fruit soup, and well it might. It sums up the light, bright and unexpected nature of this bountiful and beautiful region of France. It is a discovery well worth the making, as are all the new and exciting dishes in this chapter.

La Soupe aux Bananes

PLANTAIN AND ONION SOUP

Serves 4

The plantain, starchy relative of the banana, makes an ideal soup base, and its flavour marries superbly with the tang of curry and the mellow richness of onion.

Imperial (Metric)	American
2 fl oz (60ml) peanut oil	¼ cup peanut oil
1 large onion, sliced	1 large onion, sliced
2 cloves garlic, chopped	2 cloves garlic, chopped
8 oz (225g) sliced plantain	1½ cups sliced plantain
1 teaspoon curry powder	1 teaspoon curry powder
2 tablespoons tomato purée	2 tablespoons tomato paste
2 pints (1.2 litres) soya milk	5 cups soy milk
2 oz (50g) roasted peanuts	½ cup roasted peanuts
2 oz (50g) mango chutney	¼ cup mango chutney
Sea salt	Sea salt
Freshly ground black pepper	Freshly ground black pepper

1 Heat the oil in a large pan and sauté the onion gently until tender but not browned. Add the garlic and cook briefly.

2 Stir in the sliced plantain, curry powder and tomato purée (paste) and cook for 5 minutes, stirring frequently.

3 Place the peanuts in a blender with the milk and process briefly. Stir this mixture into the pan, bring the soup to a gentle simmer and leave to cook until the plantain is tender.

4 Place the soup in a blender and purée until smooth. Return to the pan, stir in the chutney, season to taste and reheat thoroughly.

5 Serve piping hot. Crisp celery makes a delicious accompaniment to this piquant soup.

La Soupe aux Myrtilles

BLUEBERRY SOUP

Serves 4

This soup is to be found in the Alsace and Vosges regions of France. Its light, piquant flavour makes it a pleasant dish for many occasions, including a summer breakfast. Decoctions of blueberries are traditionally supposed to cure coughs and colds, and a bowlful of this berry soup is sure to tempt even the most flagging of appetites so it is surely worth a try.

Imperial (Metric)	American
1½ lb (680g) blueberries	3 cups blueberries
½ pint (300ml) water	1⅓ cups water
3 fl oz (90ml) honey	¼ cup honey
Pinch sea salt	Pinch sea salt
Pinch cinnamon	Pinch cinnamon
¼ pint (150ml) sour cream	⅔ cup sour cream
2 tablespoons potato flour (fécule)	2 tablespoons potato starch

1 Remove all stems from the berries. Wash and drain well.

2 Place the berries in a pan with the water, honey, salt and cinnamon. Bring to the boil and cook for 5 minutes.

3 Cool the mixture slightly, then blend in a food processor. Return to the pan and reheat to boiling point.

4 In a bowl, mix together the sour cream and starch. Stir into the berry soup and boil gently for 5 minutes to cook the starch and thicken the soup.

5 Cool the soup, then chill before serving. Slices of toasted brioche are good with this dish, especially if it is being served for breakfast.

La Melonaise au Gingembre et au Coriandre

MELON AND GINGER SOUP

Serves 4

Use a scented melon, such as the Israeli Ogen, for this soup as a distinct flavour is needed to balance and harmonize with the aromatic ginger and coriander.

Imperial (Metric)	American
1 medium-sized scented melon	1 medium-sized scented melon
1 small piece fresh root ginger, peeled and grated	1 small piece fresh root ginger, peeled and grated
½ pint (300ml) white wine	1⅓ cups white wine
½ pint (300ml) natural yogurt	1⅓ cups plain yogurt
Pinch sea salt	Pinch sea salt
Sprigs of fresh coriander	Sprigs of fresh coriander
Orange peel	Orange peel

1 Halve the melon and discard the seeds. Scoop the flesh out into a blender or food processor.
2 Add the ginger, wine, yogurt and salt to the melon and blend until smooth and creamy. Chill well.
3 Ladle the chilled soup into individual glass bowls. Decorate with sprigs or coriander and *julienne* strips of orange peel. Float an ice cube in the centre of each bowl and serve at once.

Note
Melon flesh, cut into tiny balls or dice, can be added as a garnish if wished.

Crème d'Abricots aux Pistaches

APRICOT AND PISTACHIO SOUP

Serves 4

The finest French apricots come from Roussillon, Provence and the valley of the Rhône. The exotic pistachio – favourite of the Queen of Sheba – has a flavour as subtle and appealing as its soft green and russet colours.

Imperial (Metric)	American
8 oz (225g) halved and stoned ripe apricots	2 cups halved and pitted ripe apricots
½ pint (300ml) water	1⅓ cups water
2 fl oz (60ml) clear honey	2 tablespoons clear honey
2 oz (50g) pistachio kernels, skinned	½ cup pistachio kernels, skinned
½ pint (300ml) milk	1⅓ cups milk
1 oz (25g) wholemeal semolina	¼ cup whole wheat semolina
Pinch sea salt	Pinch sea salt
Pinch raw cane sugar	Pinch raw cane sugar
Pinch cinnamon or nutmeg	Pinch cinnamon or nutmeg
3 fl oz (90ml) Martini Rosso, sherry or Frontignan wine	⅓ cup Martini Rosso, sherry or Frontignan wine
Single cream (optional)	Light cream (optional)

1 Place the apricots in a large pan with the water, honey and pistachios. Bring to the boil and then simmer until the apricots are soft. Remove from the heat and process to a smooth purée.
2 Heat the milk until almost boiling. Sprinkle on the semolina, salt, sugar and spice. Cook gently for 8 minutes to thicken, stirring occasionally.
3 Stir the semolina into the fruit purée. Add the wine, stir well and reheat thoroughly. Serve hot or cold, offering a jug of cream to stir a swirl into each bowl, if wished.

La Soupe aux Pommes de Picardie

APPLE AND WALNUT SOUP WITH CALVADOS

Serves 4

There will always be debate between my homeland, France, and England, the country where I live, as to whose apples are the best. I shall stand back from the debate and merely say that, for this innovative French apple soup, sharp acidic apples are best. This soup is the epitome of the region where my ancestors lived and relatives still reside. Calvados, cider and apples all combine together – with such a wealth of variety and appeal, no wonder Adam was tempted!

Imperial (Metric)	American
1½ lb (680g) cooking apples	1½ pounds cooking apples
8 oz (225g) shelled walnuts	2 cups shelled walnuts
½ pint (300ml) dry cider	1⅓ cups hard cider
½ pint (300ml) water	1⅓ cups water
Juice of 1 orange	Juice of 1 orange
Juice of 1 lemon	Juice of 1 lemon
3 fl oz (90ml) dark, clear honey	¼ cup dark, clear honey
Pinch cinnamon	Pinch cinnamon
Pinch freshly grated nutmeg	Pinch freshly grated nutmeg
½ pint (300ml) sour cream	1⅓ cups sour cream
3 fl oz (90ml) Calvados	⅓ cup Calvados

1 Peel, core and thinly slice the apples. Place in a pan with the walnuts, cider, water, juices, honey and spices.
2 Bring the liquid to the boil and simmer gently for 15 minutes to poach the fruit.
3 Place the contents of the pan in a blender or food processor and reduce to a purée.
4 Return the mixture to the pan and reheat to boiling point. Stir in the cream and Calvados and then serve at once with toasted slices of brioche.

La Soupe à l'Avocat aux Tomates Provençales

CHILLED AVOCADO SOUP WITH TOMATOES AND BASIL

Serves 4

Avocados and tomatoes are both fruit, although we usually serve them as a savoury 'vegetable'. This soup from southern France matches the tomatoes with the richness of garlic, shallots, olive oil and basil, and pairs the avocado with creamy-sharp yogurt or fresh goat's cheese.

Imperial (Metric)	American
1 fl oz (30ml) olive oil	2 tablespoons olive oil
1 small shallot, chopped	1 small shallot, chopped
2 cloves garlic, chopped	2 cloves garlic, chopped
1 large tomato, skinned, seeded and chopped	1 large tomato, skinned, seeded and chopped
1 large avocado, stoned, peeled and chopped	1 large avocado, pitted, peeled and chopped
½ pint (300ml) water	1⅓ cups water
Sea salt	Sea salt
Freshly ground black pepper	Freshly ground black pepper
¼ pint (150ml) natural yogurt or	⅔ cup plain yogurt or fresh goat's cheese
6 oz (150ml) fresh goat's cheese	1 tablespoon snipped chives
1 tablespoon snipped chives	2 snipped basil leaves
2 snipped basil leaves	Juice of 1 lemon or 2 tablespoons cider vinegar
Juice of 1 lemon or 2 tablespoons cider vinegar	

1 Heat the oil in a large pan and sauté the shallot and garlic for 1 minute, then stir in the tomato and avocado. Cook gently for 5 minutes.

2 Add the water to the pan, bring to the boil and simmer for 4 minutes.

3 Season the mixture, place in a blender or food processor with the yogurt or goat's cheese and purée until smooth and creamy.

4 Stir in the snipped herbs and the lemon juice or vinegar. Swirl well to mix. Pour into a glass bowl and chill well before serving.

Crème d'Arachide Tropicale

PEANUT, COCONUT AND ORANGE CREAM

Serves 4

This nourishing soup of fruits and nuts has a pleasantly exotic flavour especially suited for serving chilled on a warm summer's evening. Yet the richness of flavour makes it equally delicious as a hot and creamy bowlful of goodness to warm you through on a cold winter night.

Imperial (Metric)	American
2 fl oz (60ml) vegetable oil	¼ cup vegetable oil
1 onion, chopped	1 onion, chopped
4 oz (100g) roasted peanuts	¾ cup roasted peanuts
2 oz (50g) desiccated coconut, toasted	⅔ cup desiccated coconut, toasted
8 oz (225g) skinned, seeded and chopped tomatoes	1⅓ cups skinned, seeded and chopped tomatoes
3 oranges, peeled and segmented	3 oranges, peeled and segmented
Juice of 1 orange	Juice of 1 orange
Juice of lemon	Juice of 1 lemon
2 tablespoons tomato purée	2 tablespoons tomato paste
2 pints (1.2 litres) water or vegetable stock	5 cups water or vegetable stock
Sea salt	Sea salt
Freshly ground black pepper	Freshly ground black pepper
Pinch curry powder (optional)	Pinch curry powder (optional)

1 Heat the oil in a large pan and sauté the onion until soft but not browned. Add the peanuts and coconut and cook for 2 minutes, stirring constantly.
2 Stir in the tomatoes, oranges, juices, tomato purée (paste) and water or stock. Bring to the boil, cover the pan and simmer gently for 20 minutes.
3 Pour the contents of the pan into a blender or processor and purée to a smooth cream. Season to taste with salt, pepper and curry powder if wished. Return to the pan and heat through well if serving hot. Or leave to cool and then chill well before serving cold.

La Soupe à la Bière

BEER SOUP WITH FRUIT

Serves 8

This soup is very popular in the north of France near the Belgian border, and in Alsace in eastern France, where it is made with darker beers. You can use whatever beer you prefer, but substitute malt extract for the honey if using a light ale to achieve the correct depth of flavour.

Imperial (Metric)	American
2 oz (50g) seedless raisins	⅓ cup seedless raisins
2 fl oz (60ml) malt whisky	¼ cup malt whisky
2 oz (50g) butter	¼ cup butter
2 oz (50g) wholemeal flour	½ cup whole wheat flour
2½ pints (1.4 litres) flat beer	6 cups flat beer
2 free-range egg yolks	2 free-range egg yolks
¼ pint (150ml) double cream	⅔ cup heavy cream
1 apple, cored and sliced into 8	1 apple, cored and sliced into 8
honey, to taste	honey, to taste
Sea salt	Sea salt
Freshly ground black pepper	Freshly ground black pepper
Good pinch cinnamon	Good pinch cinnamon
8 slices toasted wholemeal bread	8 slices toasted whole wheat bread
8 hop shoots, blanched (optional)	8 hop shoots, blanched (optional)

1 Soak the raisins in the whisky until needed.

2 Heat the butter in a large pan, add the flour and cook gently to form a roux.

3 Gradually stir in the beer, taking care to mix well and avoid lumps. Bring to the boil and simmer gently for 20 minutes.

4 In a bowl, mix together the egg yolks and cream. Stir in a ladleful of hot soup and mix well, then pour the mixture into the pan in a thin stream, stirring all the time.

5 Bring the soup back to the boil. When it has thickened, strain it and then reheat.

6 Add the soaked raisins and whisky to the pan. Stir in the apple slices. Simmer for 5 minutes before adding honey and seasoning.

7 Serve the soup in warmed bowls, making sure each one has a slice of apple, and garnish each with a toasted croûton of bread and a hop shoot if available.

La Soupe aux Cerises Alsacienne

RED MORELLO CHERRY SOUP

Serves 4

Cherries are native to Asia Minor, their French name deriving from Cerasus. It is thought that migratory birds first propagated this lovely fruit in other parts of the world.

Imperial (Metric)	*American*
1½ lb (650g) red Morello cherries	*4½ cups red Morello cherries*
1½ pints (850ml) red wine	*3¾ cups red wine*
3 oz (75g) honey	*¼ cup honey*
Good pinch cinnamon	*Good pinch cinnamon*
½ oz (15g) potato flour (fécule)	*1 tablespoon potato flour*
¼ pint (150ml) single cream	*⅔ cup light cream*
3 tablespoons cherry brandy	*3 tablespoons cherry brandy*
4 brioches, toasted	*4 brioches, toasted*

1 Pit the cherries. Wash well and drain.

2 Place the wine in a pan with the honey and bring to the boil. Add the cherries and cinnamon. Stew for 5 minutes, then strain the liquid into a food processor bowl.

3 Reserve a quarter of the cherries for garnish and add the rest to the bowl. Blend the rest with the wine until smooth. Return to the pan and reheat.

4 In a small bowl blend the potato flour and cream. Add gradually to the soup, stirring well. Cook for 4 minutes to thicken.

5 Stir in the whole cherries and the brandy.

6 Allow to cool, then chill well before serving with toasted brioche.

Illustrated opposite page 32.

La Soupe aux Coings

QUINCE SOUP

Serves 4

My first year of school was spent in Tarbes, where my uncle Galibert was the headmaster. My aunt took care of the huge garden at the back of the school, the pride of which were flourishing quince trees. From this fruit, which is almost inedible raw, she made excellent jellies as well as this soup. Quinces are rich in pectin which is a natural thickening, so no flour, cream or eggs are needed to give body to the soup.

Imperial (Metric)	American
2½ pints (1.4 litres) water	6 cups water
2 tea bags	2 tea bags
3 oz (75g) chopped dried peaches	½ cup chopped dried peaches
3 oz (75g) chopped dried apricots	½ cup chopped dried apricots
3 oz (75g) chopped dried apples	½ cup chopped dried apples
3 oz (75g) chopped prunes	½ cup chopped prunes
3 oz (75g) seedless raisins	½ cup seedless raisins
3 oz (75g) peeled, cored and chopped quinces	½ cup peeled, cored and chopped quinces
¼ pint (150ml) dry white wine	⅔ cup dry white wine
4 fl oz (120ml) clear honey	⅓ cup clear honey
Juice of 2 lemons	Juice of 2 lemons
¼ pint (150ml) orange juice	⅔ cup orange juice
4 oz (100g) blanched almonds	1 cup blanched almonds

1 Boil the water and brew the tea for 4 minutes before discarding the tea bags. Place the tea in a bowl and soak the dried fruits overnight.
2 Add the quinces to the bowl with the wine and honey. Place the mixture in a pan and cook gently for 30 minutes or until the fruit is completely soft.
3 Stir in the lemon and orange juice. Cool the soup before serving garnished with almonds. This soup makes a delicious breakfast, too.

La Raisinade au Yaourt

RAISIN SOUP WITH YOGURT

Serves 4

This simple and refreshing soup is a delightful appetizer for a midsummer meal. The coolness of the cucumber, the sweet tang of dried fruits, and the sharp tang of fresh coriander leaves make an unbeatable combination.

Imperial (Metric)	American
2 cucumbers, chopped	2 cucumbers, chopped
2 spring onions, chopped	2 scallions, chopped
2 oz (50g) walnut kernels	½ cup walnut kernels
2 hard-boiled free-range eggs, chopped	2 hard-cooked free-range eggs, chopped
1 clove garlic, chopped	1 clove garlic, chopped
1½ pints (850ml) natural yogurt	3¾ cups plain yogurt
½ pint (300ml) crushed ice	⅔ cup crushed ice
8 leaves fresh coriander, chopped	8 leaves fresh coriander, chopped
8 oz (225g) seedless raisins	1⅓ cups seedless raisins

1 Place all the ingredients in a blender or processor, except for half the coriander and all the raisins. Process the soup mixture until creamy.
2 Stir the raisins into the soup, cover and chill until ready to serve. Serve in chilled bowls garnished with the remaining coriander. You could float an ice cube in each bowl, too, if wished.

La Soupe Marie Stuart

HONEY-OAT SOUP WITH WILD STRAWBERRIES

Serves 4

This is a soup fit for a Queen – for Mary, Queen of Scots, who spent so much time in France, away from her true country of Scotland. This soup combines the concept of good Scottish porridge with a garnish of delicate French-style *fraises des bois*.

Imperial (Metric)	American
1½ pints (900ml) water	3¾ cups water
1 level teaspoon sea salt	1 level teaspoon sea salt
3 oz (75g) oat flakes	¾ cup oat flakes
3 oz (75g) barley flakes	¾ cup barley flakes
2 oz (50g) flaked almonds	½ cup slivered almonds
½ pint (300ml) buttermilk	1⅓ cups buttermilk
1 oz (25g) honey	1 tablespoon honey
1 pinch freshly grated nutmeg	1 pinch freshly grated nutmeg
4 oz (100g) wild strawberries	1 cup wild strawberries

1 Bring the water to the boil with the salt, then sprinkle on the flaked grains. Cook gently for 5 minutes, stirring constantly. Then remove from the heat.

2 Place the almonds in a blender with the buttermilk, honey and nutmeg. Process to a purée, then stir this mixture into the porridge.

3 Return the pan to the heat and cook, stirring, for a further 3 minutes.

4 Pour the soup into bowls and decorate with washed berries. Serve at once. This, again, is a perfect breakfast soup.

La Soupe du Paradis des Anges

HEAVENLY FRUIT SOUP

Serves 4

During my career I have travelled to many exotic countries, and have always delighted in using the produce of each region as part of my menu. Yet, until recently, most of the wonderful fruits and vegetables I had tried during my travels were unavailable outside their country of origin. How lucky are today's cooks, to be able to buy fruits and vegetables in the peak of condition, thanks to modern refrigerated transportation, without travelling further than the nearest good market!

Imperial (Metric)	American
2 fl oz (60ml) sunflower oil	¼ cup sunflower oil
1 large onion, chopped	1 large onion, chopped
2 cloves garlic, chopped	2 cloves garlic, chopped
1 green chilli, seeded and sliced	1 green chili, seeded and sliced
2 'beefsteak' tomatoes, skinned, seeded and chopped	2 large tomatoes, skinned, seeded and chopped
1 ripe avocado, stoned, peeled and chopped	1 ripe avocado, pitted, peeled and chopped
½ pint (300ml) mixed fruit juice	1⅓ cups mixed fruit juice
½ pint (300ml) water	1⅓ cups water
½ pint (300ml) buttermilk	1⅓ cups buttermilk
Sea salt	Sea salt
Freshly ground black pepper	Freshly ground black pepper

1 Heat the oil in a large soup pan. Gently sauté the onion, garlic and chilli until tender but not browned.
2 Stir in the tomatoes and avocado and cook gently, stirring, for a further 3 minutes.
3 Add the mixed fruit juices, bring to the boil and simmer for 15 minutes, then blend to a cream. Return to the pan.
4 Reheat the soup and stir in the water and buttermilk. Season to taste. Serve the soup when just at boiling point, decorated with fresh herbs.

Note
Choose freshly squeezed orange, grapefruit and lime juice as the perfect mixture for this soup.

La Turquoise du Harem

CHILLED PEACH AND ROSEPETAL CREAM SOUP

Serves 4

Once upon a time a beautiful girl was captured by marauding soldiers. They sold her to the Sultan of Istanbul, who incarcerated her for 20 years. Unlike Scheherazade she kept her captor content by cooking him wonderful meals each night, until the time when she could escape. Her name was Carmencita and her home was near the town of Conil in Andalucia, where my family lineage can be traced back to the Middle Ages. This was one of the recipes handed down by that 'jewel of the harem'.

Imperial (Metric)	American
1 cucumber, sliced	1 cucumber, sliced
6 ripe peaches, skinned, stoned and sliced	6 ripe peaches, skinned, pitted and sliced
6 walnut kernels	6 walnut kernels
6 fresh mint leaves	6 fresh mint leaves
12 scented rose petals	12 scented rose petals
2 tablespoons honey	2 tablespoons honey
Juice of 3 oranges	Juice of 3 oranges
Juice of 1 lemon	Juice of 1 lemon
6 crumbled ginger biscuits	6 crumbled ginger biscuits
½ pint (300ml) water	1⅓ cups water
½ pint (300ml) buttermilk	1⅓ cups buttermilk
Sea salt	Sea salt
Freshly ground black pepper	Freshly ground black pepper

1 Place all the ingredients in a bowl, cover and leave to marinate overnight.
2 Before serving, remove a few slices of peach for the garnish, then place the rest of the soup in a blender and process to a smooth cream. Chill well.
3 Serve the soup in chilled bowls, garnished with slices of peach and extra sprigs of mint and rose petals.

CHAPTER TWO

Les Fruits en Hors-d'Oeuvre

Fresh, Fruited Appetizers

Fruit is a traditional appetizer, but its full potential has been wasted in this respect – melon 'boats', melon and ham, grilled grapefruit, fruit juice . . . so predictable, and so dull!

In this chapter, you will find plenty to dispel the monotony of the traditional 'starter'. You can choose from dishes offering the simplicity of Banana Crisps to accompany pre-dinner drinks or the elegance of exotic ackee-filled avocado. Light, piquant – these dishes serve to whet the appetite without dulling the palate, just as the perfect appetizer should.

Of course, such dishes stem from the tradition of *haute cuisine* rather than that of French country cooking. The soups of the previous chapter are a world apart from the chic creations to be found in the following pages, splendid though they may be in their own right. The soup is a creation of the land,

and of the farmer. The appetizer is the territory of the chef, showing his or her skill in providing food which fits the seemingly contradictory criteria defined above – the 'perfect appetizer' is an elusive creation indeed.

So you will find that the dishes in this section owe more than others to the produce of France's ex-colonies. While the produce of her fields and orchards is not overlooked, it takes second place here to its more exotic second cousins – the aubergine (eggplant), avocado, mango and pawpaw (papaya). The adventurous cook takes equal delight in the familiar and the new, as does the discerning diner. Look within this selection for recipes that will waft a scent of summer islands to your table. Their effect on the appetite will be the same as that of a fresh sea breeze, giving a keen anticipation of the pleasures of the culinary delights to follow.

Les Pêches aux Airelles d'Amérique

STUFFED WHITE PEACHES WITH CRANBERRY CHEESE

Serves 4

There are enough curative elements packed into peaches and cranberries to cure a whole gamut of ailments. The leaves, bark, flowers and kernels of the peach have demulcent, sedative, diuretic and expectorant properties. Cranberries have for many years been of use in the treatment of enteritis and typhoid fever – indeed, eating cranberries with any food is a good protection against food poisoning (although this is a use seldom applied by those on a vegetarian diet!).

Imperial (Metric)	American
2 oz (50g) stoned dates, chopped	⅓ cup chopped, pitted dates
2 oz (50g) walnut kernels	½ cup walnut kernels
1 teaspoon walnut oil	1 teaspoon walnut oil
4 large white peaches	4 large white peaches
3 oz (75g) fresh goat's cheese	¾ cup fresh goat's cheese
4 fl oz (120ml) natural yogurt	½ cup plain yogurt
2 oz (50g) cranberries	½ cup cranberries
1 tablespoon ruby Port	1 tablespoon ruby Port
Pinch ground ginger	Pinch ground ginger
Pinch cinnamon	Pinch cinnamon
8 crisp lettuce leaves	8 crisp lettuce leaves

1 Place the dates, nuts and oil in a blender and reduce to a coarse paste.
2 Skin the peaches, if wished, by immersing in boiling water for 30 seconds so that the skins can be nicked and then slipped off easily. Leave the skins on if you prefer. Halve the peaches and remove the stones. Fill the cavities with the fruit and nut paste, then set aside.
3 In a bowl, beat together the cheese and yogurt until smooth.
4 Top and tail the cranberries, wash well, then place in a blender with the port. Process to a purée.
5 Beat the cranberry purée into the cheese mixture and season with ginger and cinnamon.
6 Place two lettuce leaves on each serving plate, and rest a stuffed peach half on each. Spoon a little cranberry cheese decoratively on each plate and serve the rest in individual ramekins so that bite-sized chunks of peach can be dipped before being eaten.

Jardin du Paradis

APPLE DELIGHT WITH NUTS AND BUTTERMILK

Serves 4

This delicate appetizer was created at the request of a famous film star, using some of her favourite foods. She was once amongst the ten most beautiful women in the world, now she is elderly like me – yet she retains the allure of a woman in her prime. Sadly, at her request, I cannot reveal her name . . .

Imperial (Metric)	American
4 fl oz (120ml) buttermilk	*½ cup buttermilk*
Juice of ½ an orange	*Juice of ½ an orange*
Juice of ½ a lemon	*Juice of ½ a lemon*
Sea salt	*Sea salt*
Freshly ground black pepper	*Freshly ground black pepper*
2 red-skinned apples	*2 red-skinned apples*
2 green-skinned apples	*2 green-skinned apples*
2 sticks celery	*2 stalks celery*
2 oz (50g) cashew nuts	*½ cup cashew nuts*
2 oz (50g) walnut kernels, chopped	*½ cup walnut kernels, chopped*
4 large crisp lettuce leaves	*4 large crisp lettuce leaves*
1 orange, segmented	*1 orange, segmented*
1 grapefruit, segmented	*1 grapefruit, segmented*
4 small sprigs tiny white grapes	*4 small sprigs tiny white grapes*

1 Beat together the buttermilk, fruit juices and seasoning.
2 Core and quarter the apples, then cut each quarter into thin triangular slices. Toss the slices in the buttermilk dressing and leave to marinate for 15 minutes.
3 Trim the celery then cut into very thin slices and add to the apple salad with the nuts.
4 Chill 4 shallow champagne glasses and lay a lettuce leaf in each. Spoon some of the apple salad into each, then garnish the rims of the glasses with orange and grapefuit segments. Place each glass on a serving plate and lay a sprig of grapes at the foot of each glass. Serve at once.

La Papaye à l'Enfourné

BAKED PAWPAW (PAPAYA) AU GRATIN

Serves 4

This luxurious fruit makes an imaginative and easy hot fruit appetizer. Although simple, this dish is quite rich, so follow it with a light main course – perhaps a mousse or soufflé with salad, offering fresh, crusty bread rolls for those guests with really hearty appetites.

Imperial (Metric)	American
2 green pawpaws	*2 green papayas*
Sea salt	*Sea salt*
2 oz (50g) butter	*¼ cup butter*
1 large onion, chopped	*1 large onion, chopped*
2 large tomatoes, skinned, seeded and chopped	*2 large tomatoes, skinned, seeded, and chopped*
4 oz (100g) cashew nuts, chopped	*1 cup cashew nuts, chopped*
Approx. 2 oz (50g) wholemeal breadcrumbs	*Approx. 1 cup whole wheat breadcrumbs*
Freshly ground black pepper	*Freshly ground black pepper*
4 oz (100g) grated Gruyère cheese	*1 cup grated Gruyère cheese*

1 Halve the pawpaws (papayas), scoop out the seeds and discard.
2 Bring a pan of salted water to the boil and blanch the fruit for 10 minutes. Drain and refresh in cold water.
3 While the fruit is cooking, heat the butter in a pan and sauté the onion for about 3 minutes until tender. Then stir in the tomato and nuts and simmer for about 4 minutes to thicken. If the mixture is still rather runny, add breadcrumbs to thicken. Season well.
4 Fill the pawpaw (papaya) cavities with the tomato stuffing. Place them on a baking tray and sprinkle with grated cheese. Place in a preheated oven at 400°F/200°C (Gas Mark 6) for 15 minutes, until the fruit is heated through and the cheese is sizzling and glazed. Serve at once.

Aubergine à la Noix de Coco Tonnère du Diable

SPICY BAKED AUBERGINE (EGGPLANT) WITH COCONUT MILK

Serves 4

Like tomatoes and avocados, aubergines (eggplants) are actually fruit, even though they are served in savoury dishes. Of course, unlike the other 'vegetable-fruit' mentioned, you would be hard-pressed to enjoy an aubergine (eggplant) in its raw state. Yet cooked, it is an epicurean delight.

Imperial (Metric)	*American*
2 large aubergines	*2 large eggplants*
Sea salt	*Sea salt*
2 oz (50g) butter	*¼ cup butter*
2 large onions, sliced	*2 large onions, sliced*
1 red chilli, seeded and chopped	*1 red chili, seeded and chopped*
1 pint (600ml) coconut milk	*2½ cups coconut milk*
Freshly ground black pepper	*Freshly ground black pepper*

1 Slice the aubergines (eggplants) evenly. Sprinkle with salt and leave to drain off the bitter juices for about 20 minutes. Then rinse and dry well.

2 Grease a shallow earthenware baking dish with butter, then place in the base a layer of aubergine (eggplant) slices. Cover with a layer of onion and chilli. Repeat until the layers are used up, adding a light sprinkling of seasoning each time.

3 Pour the coconut milk over the finished dish, cover with foil, then bake in a preheated oven at 400°F/ 200°C (Gas Mark 6) for 25 minutes. Remove the foil and finish baking for a further 10 minutes to brown lightly.

4 Cook for a few minutes before cutting into squares and serving with whole wheat bread as a hearty appetizer, or even as a meal in itself with a pulse-based salad.

Banane Pesée Frite

BANANA CRISPS

Serves 4

In all the islands of the French Caribbean you will find these delicious and unusual crisps served with drinks – you could choose from the exciting selection in Chapter Ten if you wish to create a Caribbean atmosphere for a cocktail party.

Imperial (Metric)	*American*
1 lb (450g) bananas or plantains	*1 pound bananas or plantains*
Sea salt	*Sea salt*
Vegetable oil for deep frying	*Vegetable oil for deep frying*

1 Peel the bananas, cut into slices ⅓ inch (1cm) thick and soak in a bowl of cold salted water for 30 minutes. Drain and pat dry.

2 Fill a large pan two-thirds full of oil and heat to a temperature of 375°F/190°C.

3 Fry the banana slices a few at a time for 2 minutes. They should be golden but not over-browned. Scoop out with a slotted spoon and drain well on absorbent paper.

4 When all the banana slices have been cooked, lay a sheet of greaseproof (parchment) paper over them and press until they are halved in thickness.

5 Dip the pressed slices in salted water, drain and pat dry again, then re-fry until they are crisp and golden-brown. Drain well on fresh sheets of absorbent paper towel. Serve with a selection of dips and cocktails.

Opposite Red Morello Cherry Soup (page 21).

Souscaille

A MANGO APPETIZER FROM MARTINIQUE

Serves 4

Fresh mangoes are becoming increasingly popular as the basis for a light meal, especially with salads or fish. In this instance it captures the appetite all by itself, with just a piquant dressing to bring out its natural flavours.

Imperial (Metric)	*American*
2 large green mangoes	*2 large green mangoes*
¼ pint (150ml) tomato juice	*⅔ cup tomato juice*
2 cloves garlic, chopped	*2 cloves garlic, chopped*
1 green pepper, seeded and chopped	*1 green pepper, seeded and chopped*
Juice of 1 lime	*Juice of 1 lime*
1 tablespoon clear honey	*1 tablespoon clear honey*
Sea salt	*Sea salt*
Freshly ground black pepper	*Freshly ground black pepper*

1 Peel and thinly slice the mangoes, and place the slices in a shallow bowl.
2 Place the tomato juice, garlic, green pepper and lime juice in a blender and reduce to a smooth purée. Season to taste with honey, salt and pepper.
3 Pour the sauce over the mango slices and leave to marinate for at least 20 minutes.
4 Serve the mango slices on individual plates. Sprigs of fresh coriander would make a pleasant garnish, and thinly sliced whole wheat bread, lightly buttered, could be offered as well.

Opposite Holyland Melon with Cheese Mousse and Raspberries (page 40).

Les Concombres à l'Orange

CUCUMBER IN A SPICY ORANGE MARINADE

Serves 4

A simple creation, but how much more exciting than the usual *raita* as a cooling Summer salad – and how much prettier, with pale greens and golds softened by a wash of carrot-tinted buttermilk.

Imperial (Metric)	American
1 cucumber, peeled	2 cucumbers, peeled
2 large oranges	2 large oranges
1 tablespoon clear honey	1 tablespoon clear honey
1 grapefruit	1 grapefruit
1 cooked carrot	1 cooked carrot
¼ pint (150ml) buttermilk	⅔ cup buttermilk
1 small piece fresh, peeled ginger	1 small piece fresh, peeled ginger
Sea salt	Sea salt
Freshly ground black pepper	Freshly ground black pepper

1 Split the cucumber lengthwise and slice it across into ¼-inch (5mm) moons. Place in a large salad bowl.

2 Using a zester, peel some fine ribbons of outer peel from one of the oranges. Blanch in boiling water for 10 minutes, then drain. Place the blanched zest in a small bowl with the honey.

3 While the zest is being blanched, carefully peel the oranges and grapefruit, removing all the pith, and cut into segments. Do this over a bowl, so that any juice is collected. Place the segments in the salad bowl with the cucumber.

4 Pour the juice into a blender. Scrape and chop the carrot, and add this too. Pour in the buttermilk, and add the ginger. Blend until smooth, then season to taste.

5 Pour this dressing over the cucumber and citrus fruit, and toss well.

6 Spoon the salad into individual bowls, or onto plates lined with curly endive (chicory). Sprinkle each portion with honeyed orange zest, then serve.

Tomate Picasso

TOMATO WITH A CREAMY AVOCADO-EGG FILLING

Serves 2

There are so many shapes, sizes and colours of tomato, that it is easy to find just the type you need to complement any dish. For this one, choose large, flavoursome ribbed fruits – but steer clear of watery, mushy, smooth-sided giants which have no flavour and will only serve to water down the light and mellow-flavoured stuffing.

Imperial (Metric)	American
2 large tomatoes	*2 large tomatoes*
1 oz (25g) butter	*2 tablespoons butter*
3 eggs, beaten	*3 eggs, beaten*
2 tablespoons natural yogurt	*2 tablespoons plain yogurt*
1 ripe avocado	*1 ripe avocado*
1 spring onion, finely chopped	*1 scallion, finely chopped*
Sea salt	*Sea salt*
Freshly ground black pepper	*Freshly ground black pepper*
2 tablespoons olive oil	*2 tablespoons olive oil*
1 teaspoon fresh chopped parsley	*1 teaspoon fresh chopped parsley*
Wedges of fresh lime, to serve	*Wedges of fresh lime, to serve*

1 Trim the 'eye' from around the stem of each tomato and make two nicks in the skin of each, at the sides. Scald them for 20 seconds in boiling water, then drain. Peel off the skins.

2 Stand the tomatoes, stem side down, on a clean surface. Cut a small lid off each and scoop out the centres. Reserve the flesh. Now turn the tomatoes upside-down so that any excess juice may drain out.

3 Place the tomato flesh in a blender. Purée, then sieve it into a pan. Boil gently for 5 minutes, then set aside to cool.

4 Heat the butter in a small pan, then stir in the eggs and yogurt. Cook very, very gently until they are a creamy scramble, then turn into a bowl.

5 Halve the avocado and cut one half into small dice. Keep the stone in the other half and cover in clingfilm (Saran wrap). Stir the diced avocado into the egg mixture, along with the chopped onion (scallion). Season to taste.

6 Spoon the mixture into the upturned tomato shells and place each one on a serving plate.

7 Stir the oil into the tomato pulp and season to taste. Drizzle this dressing over the tomatoes and sprinkle with parsley. Peel and slice the remaining avocado and decorate the plates with this and the lime wedges. Serve at once, with the filling just lukewarm or at room temperature.

Les Oeufs de Cailles au Kiwi

QUAILS' EGGS IN A KIWI FRUIT NEST
Serves 4

The kiwi fruit has been the subject of derision of late, because of its omnipresence as a garnish on the plates of the smartest restaurants. And yet, it deserves more credibility than it has received – it is extremely high in vitamin C, and it has a protein-digesting enzyme similar to that found in papaya. It is also delicious, especially in this exquisite chutney, which can be stored in sterilized jars in the refrigerator as a delicious adjunct to all sorts of dishes. Use firm fruit for best results.

Imperial (Metric)	American
For the chutney	**For the chutney**
6 kiwi fruit, peeled and diced	6 kiwi fruit, peeled and diced
1 medium onion, peeled and chopped	1 medium onion, peeled and chopped
1 clove garlic, crushed	1 clove garlic, crushed
3 oz (75g) dried dates, chopped	½ cup chopped dried dates
1 small piece fresh ginger, chopped	1 small piece fresh ginger, chopped
5 oz (150g) Demerara sugar	Scant cup raw cane sugar
¼ pint (150ml) cider vinegar	⅔ cup cider vinegar
1 green chilli, seeded and chopped	1 green chili, seeded and chopped
2 chopped mint leaves	2 chopped mint leaves
Sea salt	Sea salt
Freshly ground black pepper	Freshly ground black pepper
12 quails' eggs	12 quail's eggs
1 tea bag	1 tea bag
1 small pickled beetroot	1 small pickled beet
1 stick celery	1 stalk celery
8 walnut kernels	8 walnut kernels
4 sprigs lamb's lettuce	4 sprigs corn salad
4 peeled slices kiwi fruit	4 peeled slices kiwi fruit

1 To make the chutney, place all the ingredients except seasoning in a pan and stew gently for about 20 minutes, stirring occasionally, until the right consistency is achieved. Season to taste. Allow to cool.
2 Boil the eggs in salted water for 5 minutes. Turn off the heat and remove the eggs, crack them gently all over, then return them to the pan along with the tea bag. Leave in the brew for 10 minutes before shelling. The subtle crackle produced by the tea on the whites has a delicate, Oriental look.
3 Cut the beetroot (beet) and the celery into fine julienne strips, and roughly chop the nuts.

4 Spoon a generous mound of kiwi chutney onto four individual plates, then arrange the julienned vegetables and chopped nuts around it, like a nest.

5 Gently press three eggs into each nest. Decorate the plates with sprigs of lamb's lettuce and slices of kiwi fruit, then serve.

La Figue au Fromage de Chèvre
FRESH FIGS WITH TOASTED GOAT'S CHEESE

Serves 4

The many colours of fig all have their special fans in France. Some like the white bourgassote, aubique, blanquette and courelle, others the pink date fig or violet dauphin. But I believe the best are the black bernissenque, sultane and the Versailles. When I was a child in my Uncle's school, the fig tree that overhung our playground provided us with the finest missiles – great juicy projectiles that splashed colour and aroma with every direct hit! Don't waste these luscious fruit the way we children did, but choose ripe examples for this simple appetizer.

Imperial (Metric)	American
4 slices goat's cheese	*4 slices goat's cheese*
4 slices toasted brioche	*4 slices toasted brioche*
1 tablespoon walnut oil	*1 tablespoon walnut oil*
8 oz (225g) raspberries	*2 cups raspberries*
1 tablespoon Martini Rosé	*1 tablespoon Martini Rosé*
2 oz (50g) cooked apple slices	*½ cup cooked apple slices*
Freshly ground black pepper	*Freshly ground black pepper*
8 ripe black figs	*8 ripe black figs*

1 Lay the slices of goat's cheese over the brioche slices. Brush the cheese with walnut oil. Heat the grill (broiler).

2 Place the raspberries, Martini and apples in a blender. Blend until smooth, then pass through a strainer into a bowl. Season with black pepper and set aside.

3 Place the goat's cheese brioches under the grill (broiler).

4 Cut crosses in the tops of the figs, and push them gently open.

5 Spoon a little sauce onto each of four plates, then set a sizzling goat's cheese croûton on each. Place two figs beside each croûton and serve immediately.

L'Avocat Farçi au Fruit Défendu

AVOCADO FILLED WITH ACKEE

Serves 4

Ackee is a wonderful fruit, yet it is still relatively unknown. Its Latin name, *Blighia sapidia* is a clue to its discoverer – Captain Bligh, no less, who introduced it to Jamaica where it has become a valued ingredient. I developed this dish at the Frenchman's Cove Hotel on that beautiful island, and it will always bring with it the heady atmosphere of the tropics for me. You will be lucky to find fresh ackee, but it is more readily obtained in cans, and is very good in this form. Vegans may already be aware of the 'scrambled egg' flavour and consistency of ackee – if not, they have a treat in store!

Imperial (Metric)	American
2 tablespoons vegetable oil	2 tablespoons vegetable oil
1 medium onion, finely chopped	1 medium onion, finely chopped
1 teaspoon curry powder	1 teaspoon curry powder
1 tablespoon tomato purée	1 tablespoon tomato paste
1 teaspoon flour	1 teaspoon flour
¼ pint (150ml) coconut milk	⅔ cup coconut milk
8 oz (225g) drained canned ackee	1 cup drained canned ackee
Sea salt	Sea salt
Freshly ground black pepper	Freshly ground black pepper
Juice of 1 lime	Juice of 1 lime
2 ripe avocados	2 ripe avocados

1 Heat the oil in a saucepan and sauté the onion for 3 minutes, then stir in the curry powder and cook gently to release the aromatic oils. Stir in the flour and the tomato purée (paste). Mix well, then gradually add the coconut milk. Simmer for 12 minutes, stirring frequently.
2 Add the ackees to the pan and cook until completely warmed through. The mixture should be thick and unctious, like soft scrambled eggs. Season to taste and keep warm.
3 Halve the avocados, remove the stones and place in individual bowls. Immediately, stir the lime juice into the hot ackee mixture and spoon this into the avocados. The combination of cool avocado and hot ackee is exceptional. Slices of chilled mango make a delicious accompaniment.

Note
Coconut Milk: *Infuse 1 oz (25g) desiccated coconut in 4½ fl oz (125ml) boiling water. Liquidize and strain.*

Les Letchis aux Amandes

LYCHEES, STUFFED WITH A FIG AND ALMOND PASTE

Serves 4

This recipe also uses figs, but in their dried form as part of a simple yet delicious mincemeat that fills silken lychees before they become part of a crisp, fresh salad. A dressing with an Oriental flavour completes this original presentation.

Imperial (Metric)	American
8 fresh lychees	8 fresh lychees
3 oz (75g) flaked almonds	¾ cup slivered almonds
2 oz (50g) dried figs	Scant ½ cup dried figs
1 teaspoon orange liqueur	1 teaspoon orange liqueur
2 heads chicory, shredded	2 heads Belgian endive, shredded
6 oz (150g) mangetouts, blanched	1 cup snow peas, blanched
1 spring onion, thinly sliced	1 scallion, thinly sliced
1 teaspoon soya sauce	1 teaspoon soy sauce
1 small piece fresh ginger, chopped	1 small piece fresh ginger, chopped
3 fl oz (90ml) pineapple juice	⅓ cup pineapple juice
2 fl oz (60ml) sesame oil	¼ cup sesame oil
Sea salt	Sea salt
Freshly ground black pepper	Freshly ground black pepper

1 Peel and pit the lychees. Place the almonds, figs and liqueur in a blender and reduce to a stiff paste. Use this to stuff the lychees, then set aside.

2 Place the vegetables in a large bowl.

3 Place the remaining ingredients in a blender and blend to a smooth dressing, then drizzle this over the vegetables and toss well to coat them all.

4 Arrange the salad on a plate like a nest, in which you can then nestle the stuffed lychees like piquant eggs. Serve at once.

Melon de la Terre Sainte en Parade

HOLYLAND MELON WITH CHEESE MOUSSE AND RASPBERRIES

Serves 4

One of the most refreshing and delicious drinks I have ever tasted consisted simply of the pulp of an Ogen melon, liquidized with a dash of dry vermouth or gin. This, served in a tall glass, with a few raspberries floating on top, would serve to lift the spirit on even the most dreary of days.

This dish, with its balance of scented melon, fruity raspberries and light, creamy cheese, is equally appealing. It is given here as an appetizer, but it would make a splendid light Summer lunch, especially for those watching their weight.

Imperial (Metric)	*American*
2 medium Ogen melons	*2 medium Ogen melons*
6 oz (150g) low-fat soft cheese	*¾ cup low-fat soft cheese*
1 hard-boiled egg, shelled	*1 hard-cooked egg, shelled*
1 teaspoon dry vermouth	*1 teaspoon dry vermouth*
Pinch cayenne pepper	*Pinch cayenne pepper*
8 oz (225g) fresh raspberries	*2 cups fresh raspberries*

1 Halve the melons, scoop out and discard the seeds. Use a Parisienne cutter to scoop small balls of fruit from the melons. Reserve the melon balls and place the shells in individual bowls.

2 Mash together the cheese and the chopped egg. Pass through a sieve (strainer) if necessary to obtain a well-blended mixture. Mix in the vermouth and season with a little cayenne. Shape the mixture into balls of the same size as the melon pieces.

3 Wash and drain the raspberries. Into each melon half place a balanced mixture of melon, cheese and raspberries, paying attention to colour and presentation. No dressing is needed. Decorate as wished with a sprig or two of apple mint, then serve.

Illustrated opposite page 33.

CHAPTER THREE

Les Salades Fruitières aux Herbes

Salads of Fruits and Greenery

For many years, the salad was a sorry item. Hardly more than a garnish, it usually consisted of a few limp leaves, a slice or two of tomato and cucumber, and perhaps another sad vegetable or two, swamped with artificial-flavoured salad cream. It was every child's dread, and for adults it was something to be endured by dieters as part of the penance for eating too much or too well of other, fattening, forbidden fruit.

More recently, it has been elevated to dizzy heights by the advent of the new style of cooking. The *salade tiède* was the epitome of chic food: 'and I intend to stick to it until my customers get fed up with it!' cried one colleague to me. So the poor diner went from one extreme to the other. From salad as an oversight to salad as a fine art. Is either one the right way to regard good, fresh food in the peak of its natural, raw state? I think not.

However, at least *nouvelle cuisine* has had its benefits. It has introduced to our plates (or perhaps reintroduced) the sheer creativity of the salad dish. It has championed the use of unusual ingredients – a wealth of different leaves, the fresh taste of herbs, the combination of proteins in the dish to make the salad as much a separate course as the appetizer or the entrée. It has offered a choice between the traditional oil and vinegar or mayonnaise dressing and the new low-fat combinations of yogurt, nut oils, fruit juices and other, flavourful ingredients, making the dressing as important a part of the salad as the leaves themselves. And not least it has brought fruit back into the equation, playing a splendid leading role in the salads of today.

So our salads have become amongst the most exciting food options available today. They can balance the most stimulating mixtures of flavours, textures, colours and aromas, with each ingredient shining through whilst harmonizing with the rest. There is a freedom of creativity which seems to me to epitomize the youthful vigour of the new health movement.

41

It is this spirit of creativity which has led me, just for fun, to dedicate the salads in this chapter to some of the great French artists of the past – writers, painters and poets. I feel that each one would have relished the dish which I have linked with his name. My one exception is the salad on page 58, which I have dedicated to the lady who has been my own inspiration and mainstay for many years. I know she will not be daunted at being in such lofty company, for her vitality and spirit outshines them all.

La Salade de la Fontaine

A SALAD OF VEGETABLE, FRUIT AND NUT

Serves 4

Jean de la Fontaine was the storyteller of the period of Louis XIV, and his fables have been loved by French children over the generations. A favourite of mine used to be *La Cigale et la Fourmi* – the Cicada and the Ant. It is winter, and the hungry cicada asks for food from the industrious ant. 'But what were you doing last summer?' asks the ant, who had spent that season gathering food. 'I sang!' replies the cicada, loftily. 'Indeed,' replies the ant, 'then dance now.' If, like me, you find the creation of good food as much of a joy as music and dance, then we can think ourselves fortunate in combining work with pleasure.

Imperial (Metric)
For the dressing
4 fl oz (120ml) buttermilk
1 teaspoon Dijon mustard
1 teaspoon honey
3 tablespoons cider vinegar
2 oz (50g) toasted hazelnuts
1 shallot, finely chopped
Sea salt
Freshly ground black pepper

For the salad
1 lb (450g) white cabbage
2 green apples
4 oz (100g) seedless raisins
4 oz (100g) toasted hazelnuts
4 oz (100g) blueberries
5 oz (125g) chopped pineapple

American
For the dressing
½ cup buttermilk
1 teaspoon Dijon mustard
1 teaspoon honey
3 tablespoons cider vinegar
½ cup toasted hazelnuts
1 shallot, finely chopped
Sea salt
Freshly ground black pepper

For the salad
1 pound white cabbage
2 green apples
⅔ cup seedless raisins
1 cup toasted hazelnuts
1 cup blueberries
1 cup chopped pineapple

1 Place all the dressing ingredients in a blender and process to a smooth cream.
2 Core and shred the cabbage. Core and quarter the apples, then cut into thin triangles. Toss the cabbage and apple in half the dressing and leave to macerate for 30 minutes.
3 Place the apple and cabbage mixture in a bowl and toss with the raisins, nuts, berries and pineapple. Serve the rest of the dressing separately. This salad looks especially pretty if decorated with tiny blue borage flowers.

La Salade Paul et Rose Cézanne

A MERIDIONAL SALAD WITH OLIVES

Serves 4

Paul Cézanne's sister Rose married Maxime Conil in 1881, and the great impressionist painter often visited the Conil estate at Montbriant where he could gaze upon the Arc valley with Mont Sainte-Victoire and the fine railway viaduct, background to one of his paintings. Paul and Maxime used to argue, and Cézanne once wrote to Emile Zola that Maxime's only talent was to select the olives for a salad – he was too much of a bon viveur for Paul's liking! In this letter he included a snatch of verse about his brother-in-law:

'O fils dégénéré, tu fais ici la noce!
Hélas! Ton habit neuf est tout taché de sauce,
. . . Abjure les liqueurs, c'est trés pernicieux
et ne bois que l'eau, tu t'en trouveras mieux.'

Translation
Oh degenerate son, thou art overly enjoying thyself!
Alas! Your new suit is all stained with sauce,
. . . Forswear all liqueur, it is pernicious
and let water be your only drink, for then you will enjoy good health.

Imperial (Metric) **For the dressing**	*American* **For the dressing**
3 tablespoons olive oil	*3 tablespoons olive oil*
2 tablespoons wine vinegar	*2 tablespoons wine vinegar*
2 oz (50g) fresh goat's cheese	*¼ cup fresh goat's cheese*
1 teaspoon Dijon mustard	*1 teaspoon Dijon mustard*
Sea salt	*Sea salt*
Freshly ground black pepper	*Freshly ground black pepper*

1 Place all the dressing ingredients in a blender and blend until smooth.

For the salad

1 head curly endive
12 sprigs corn salad
6 cloves garlic, finely chopped
8 oz (225g) French beans, blanched
5 oz (125g) croûtons
5 oz (125g) walnuts
8 oz (225g) mixed green and black olives, stoned
6 hard-boiled eggs, sliced
3 large ribbed tomatoes, sliced

For the salad

1 head curly chicory
12 sprigs lamb's lettuce
6 cloves garlic, finely chopped
2 cups snap beans, blanched
1 cup croûtons
1 cup walnuts
2 cups mixed green and black olives, pitted
6 hard-cooked eggs, sliced
3 large ribbed tomatoes, sliced

2 Separate the salad leaves and wash well. Drain thoroughly. Place in a large bowl with the chopped garlic, beans, croûtons, nuts and olives. Toss well, then drizzle with most of the dressing and toss again.

3 Place the salad in individual serving bowls or one large bowl and decorate with slices of egg and tomato. Drizzle the last of the dressing over the slices, then serve at once.

La Salade Molière

BEAN AND CHERRY TOMATO SALAD WITH A FLORAL GARNISH

Serves 4

We have all experienced that rare meal with a host whose hospitality is not quite what it should be. Molière had a fine grasp of the nature of human avarice, and in one piece a character instructs his cook to prepare lots of bean dishes for the guests to fill them up so that they will not ask for other, more luxurious and expensive foods.

Now, of course, we know the high-fibre benefits of pulses, and their filling effect has been the key to many a successful diet. This dish, served as a main-course salad for 4 or an appetizer for 6, can be either filling or appetite-whetting according to your requirements. And so pretty is it, with its rainbow colours, that it is a joy in itself.

Imperial (Metric)	American
For the dressing	**For the dressing**
Juice of 1 grapefruit	Juice of 1 grapefruit
3 fl oz (90ml) natural yogurt	⅓ cup plain yogurt
5 leaves fresh basil	5 leaves fresh basil
5 walnut kernels	5 walnut kernels
Sea salt	Sea salt
Freshly ground black pepper	Freshly ground black pepper
For the salad	**For the salad**
8 oz (225g) fresh flageolet beans	1¼ cups fresh flageolet beans
8 oz (225g) fresh broad beans	1½ cups fresh Lima beans
8 oz (225g) cherry tomatoes	8 ounces cherry tomatoes
8 black olives, stoned	8 black olives, pitted
2 spring onions	2 scallions
2 tablespoons chopped parsley	2 tablespoons chopped parsley
Marigold petals, to garnish	Marigold petals, to garnish

1 Place all the ingredients for the dressing in a blender and blend until smooth. Set aside for the flavours to develop and mingle.
2 Boil the beans in unsalted water for 20 minutes, or until tender. Peel away any tough outer skins and leave the beans to cool slightly, then toss in one-third of the dressing and reserve.
3 Scald the tomatoes briefly in boiling water and peel off the skins.
4 Arrange the beans in the centre of a large glass plate. Arrange tomatoes and olives around them.

5 Slice the onions (scallions) diagonally and sprinkle them over the beans. Sprinkle parsley over the tomatoes and olives, and marigold petals over the beans. Serve at once, offering extra dressing in a glass jug.

Note
In the past, cowslips would have been used instead of marigold petals, but cowslips are now so rare and precious that they should be cherished in the wild. The charming, bright little marigold that adorns our gardens so freely is a pretty and worthy substitute.

La Salade Edmond Rostand

A RICH RICE SALAD WITH ARTICHOKES AND NASTURTIUM FLOWERS

Serves 4

Rostand's poignant hero Cyrano de Bergerac epitomized the bravado inherent in all Frenchmen. In recent years he has become known only as the owner of a somewhat oversized nose yet, when staged, the play featuring this great character is hailed by the critics. And the ladies? Well, they still fall for Cyrano because, as any Frenchman will tell you, it is poetry that wins genuine affection, not a handsome face.

But equally French is the understanding of food as an aperitif to love. So this splendid salad is named for the creator of the noble Cyrano. In the name of love, you may omit the garlic!

Imperial (Metric)	American
For the dressing	**For the dressing**
2 oz (50g) flaked almonds	½ cup slivered almonds
Juice of 1 lemon	Juice of 1 lemon
1 tablespoon white wine vinegar	1 tablespoon white wine vinegar
1 shallot, finely chopped	1 shallot, finely chopped
1 clove garlic (optional)	1 clove garlic (optional)
1 oz (25g) tomato purée	2 tablespoons tomato paste
3 fl oz (90ml) buttermilk	⅓ cup buttermilk
Sea salt	Sea salt
Freshly ground black pepper	Freshly ground black pepper
For the salad	**For the salad**
8 oz (225g) rice, cooked	1 cup rice, cooked
4 large crisp lettuce leaves	4 large crisp lettuce leaves
6 cooked artichoke bottoms, diced	6 cooked artichoke bottoms, diced
12 seedless green grapes	12 seedless green grapes
Chopped fresh coriander or chervil and nasturtium flowers, to garnish	Chopped fresh coriander or chervil and nasturtium flowers, to garnish

1 Place all the ingredients for the dressing in a blender and blend to produce an almond flavoured dressing.

2 Toss the rice in half the dressing. Lay a lettuce leaf on each of four small salad plates, then spoon a little of the rice onto each.

3 Arrange artichokes and grapes over each portion and then sprinkle with the garnishes. Serve the remaining dressing separately.

Variation
For a more substantial salad, add chopped hard-boiled egg to the finished dish.

La Salade Honoré de Balzac

WATERMELON AND CUCUMBER SALAD IN A BUTTERMILK DRESSING

Serves 4

It is with wry humour that I name this delicate, light salad for such a noted trencherman. It was nothing for the author of *La Comédie Humaine* to devour a dozen cutlets, a half-dozen roasted quails and perhaps the best part of a wheel of Brie with six baguettes at a single sitting. The salad was a mere interlude! No wonder that it is said he encouraged the great chef Carême, helping in the writing and editing of his six cookery books. Far from the starving artist, perhaps Balzac might have benefited from a taste of *nouvelle cuisine* once in a while – what a revelation it would have been!

Imperial (Metric)	American
For the dressing	**For the dressing**
4 fl oz (120ml) buttermilk	*½ cup buttermilk*
A few sprigs of chives, chopped	*A few sprigs of chives, chopped*
4 hard-boiled eggs, chopped	*4 hard-cooked eggs, chopped*
Sea salt	*Sea salt*
Freshly ground black pepper	*Freshly ground black pepper*
For the salad	**For the salad**
1 small watermelon	*1 small watermelon*
1 cucumber	*2 cucumbers*
1 lb (450g) lamb's lettuce	*1 pound corn salad*
Courgette flowers, for garnish	*Courgette flowers, for garnish*

1 Place the ingredients for the dressing in a blender and blend until smooth. If the mixture is too thick, add a little more buttermilk, but it should be creamy and clinging to suit its purpose.

2 Cut the melon into small triangular wedges. Leave the seeds in – they are as nutritious as they are decorative.

3 Peel and chop the cucumber and mix with half the dressing. Reserve the rest of the dressing to serve separately.

4 Separate the leaves of the lettuce, wash and drain well.

5 Make a bed of leaves on a large plate and spoon the cucumber mixture into the centre. Decorate the dish with the melon wedges, spiked in amongst the leaves like jewels. A few washed courgette flowers, arranged around the edge, are the finishing touch. This simple salad is an excellent accompaniment to grilled or barbecued vegetables or fish as a Summer lunch on the lawn or beach.

La Salade Victor Hugo

CHERRY AND WALNUT SALAD WITH ORANGE

Serves 4

What a different world it was for Hugo's hero, Jean Valjean, who stole a loaf of bread to feed his starving family and was sentenced to life imprisonment on the notorious Guyanne island. We find it hard to believe that such a minor crime could warrant so major a punishment. But, as our grain mountains grow higher while people still starve to death, perhaps we have only exchanged one topsy-turvey situation for another?

Imperial (Metric)	*American*
For the dressing	**For the dressing**
3 tablespoons hazelnut oil	*3 tablespoons hazelnut oil*
1 tablespoon cider vinegar	*1 tablespoon cider vinegar*
1 teaspoon Dijon mustard	*1 teaspoon Dijon mustard*
Sea salt	*Sea salt*
Freshly ground black pepper	*Freshly ground black pepper*
For the salad	**For the salad**
1 orange	*1 orange*
12 oz (350g) red or black cherries	*2 cups red or black cherries*
2 oz (50g) pistachio kernels	*½ cup pistachio kernels*
1 Cos lettuce	*1 Romaine lettuce*

1 Place all the ingredients for the dressing in a screw-capped jar. Put the lid on tightly, then shake well to blend everything to an emulsion.

2 Over a shallow bowl, cut the peel and pith from the orange and cut the orange into thin circles. Pour any juice collected into the jar of dressing.

3 Wash, halve and pit the cherries, reserving just a few pairs on stalks as a garnish. Chop the nuts roughly.

4 Tear the lettuce into bite-sized pieces and arrange around the edge of a serving dish. Lay the orange slices in the centre.

5 Shake the dressing again to blend. Put the cherries in a bowl, and toss with a little of the dressing. Pile over the orange slices and sprinkle with chopped pistachios.

6 Drizzle a little more dressing over the lettuce, then serve the dish, garnished with the whole cherries.

La Salade Jean-Jacques Rousseau

AN EXOTIC SALAD WITH STIR-FRIED MUSHROOMS

Serves 4

Rousseau was a revolutionary thinker in many ways, not least in terms of diet. He believed that it was not human nature to eat meat, pointing out that children tended to dislike meat until conditioned to eat it by their parents. He believed meat-eaters to be crueller, too, than vegetarians. His views on diet were linked to his perceptions of the inequality of French society, in which the rich 'cannibalized' the poor. How astonishing to realize that the man who engineered the principles of the French Revolution was even then putting forward ideas that we are only now coming to discover for ourselves . . .

Imperial (Metric)	American
For the dressing	**For the dressing**
1 peeled kiwi fruit	*1 peeled kiwi fruit*
3 fl oz (90ml) natural yogurt	*⅓ cup plain yogurt*
1 tablespoon cider vinegar	*1 tablespoon cider vinegar*
1 tablespoon grapefruit juice	*1 tablespoon grapefruit juice*
2 oz (50g) flaked almonds	*½ cup slivered almonds*
Sea salt	*Sea salt*
Freshly ground black pepper	*Freshly ground black pepper*
1 teaspoon honey	*1 teaspoon honey*
For the salad	**For the salad**
8 oz (225g) beansprouts	*½ pound beansprouts*
1 head chicory, sliced	*1 head Belgian endive, sliced*
1 grapefruit, peeled and segmented	*1 grapefruit, peeled and segmented*
8 lychees, peeled and pitted	*8 lychees, peeled and pitted*
5 oz (125g) mooli radish, thinly sliced	*1 heaping cup thinly sliced mooli radish*
For the stir-fry	**For the stir-fry**
2 tablespoons olive oil	*2 tablespoons olive oil*
1 shallot, finely chopped	*1 shallot, finely chopped*
2 cloves garlic, crushed	*2 cloves garlic, crushed*
8 oz (225g) sliced field mushrooms	*4 cups sliced field mushrooms*

1 Place all the ingredients for the dressing in a blender and process to a smooth cream. Set aside for the flavours to mingle.

2 Place all the salad ingredients in a large, shallow bowl (you could halve the lychees first, if wished). Toss with the dressing.

3 Heat the oil in a pan and sauté the shallot and garlic until tender but not browned. Then add the mushrooms and sauté very briefly.

4 Spoon the stir-fry mixture over the salad and serve at once.

La Salade Baudelaire

CAULIFLOWER FLORETS IN A SPICY DRESSING

Serves 4

In Baudelaire's time the restaurants of the Latin Quarter were full of pretty girls and starving students. Things were not so different when I attended the College Stanislas there, nor when I worked at La Coupole under Monsieur Lafon. Forty years later, my wife and I went to visit him there, and he was still as fresh and vigorous at eighty as he had been all those years before. He treated us royally, and so I offer this recipe, created in the spirit of his truly Parisien restaurant with my very grateful thanks.

Imperial (Metric)	*American*
For the dressing	**For the dressing**
4 fl oz (120ml) natural yogurt	*½ cup plain yogurt*
3 fl oz (90ml) tomato juice	*⅓ cup tomato juice*
2 tablespoons cider vinegar	*2 tablespoons cider vinegar*
1 tablespoon Dijon mustard	*1 tablespoon Dijon mustard*
1 teaspoon curry powder	*1 teaspoon curry powder*
3 oz (75g) roasted peanuts	*½ cup roasted peanuts*
1 teaspoon honey	*1 teaspoon honey*
Dash Tabasco sauce	*Dash Tabasco sauce*
Sea salt	*Sea salt*
Freshly ground black pepper	*Freshly ground black pepper*
For the salad	**For the salad**
1 medium cauliflower	*1 medium cauliflower*
8 spring onions	*8 scallions*
8 small mushrooms	*8 small mushrooms*
5 oz (125g) seedless raisins	*¾ cup seedless raisins*

1 Place all the ingredients for the dressing in a blender and blend until smooth. Set aside until needed.

2 Break the cauliflower into small florets and blanch these in boiling water for 3 minutes. Drain well, then place in a large bowl.

3 Trim the spring onions (scallions) and cut into small pieces. Place in the bowl.

4 Trim and quarter the mushrooms and add to the bowl, along with the raisins.

5 Pour the dressing over the salad and toss well. Leave to marinate for at least 2 hours before serving. This salad is delicious served on a bed of watercress. It can also be served with good, strong cheese and crusty French bread as a sort of pickle.

La Salade André Simon

APRICOT AND POTATO SALAD WITH WATERCRESS

Serves 4

In 1949, with the help of Marius Dutrey who had been head chef of the Savoy Hotel, and Signor B Calderoni of the Normandy Hotel, I founded the famous Academy of Chefs de Cuisine. The first President d'Honneur was André Simon who gave me his wholehearted support and blessing, and we remained in close contact until his death. This great man is owed a debt of gratitude by every gourmet for his contribution to gastronomy – his formidable range of books on good food and wine still sets a standard to which every food writer aspires. Here is a small tribute from a humble chef, in admiration of his work.

Imperial (Metric)	*American*
For the dressing	**For the dressing**
3 fl oz (90ml) buttermilk	*⅓ cup buttermilk*
3 tablespoons dry white wine	*3 tablespoons dry white wine*
1 teaspoon honey	*1 teaspoon honey*
1 teaspoon grainy mustard	*1 teaspoon grainy mustard*
2 finely chopped spring onions	*2 finely chopped scallions*
Sea salt	*Sea salt*
Freshly ground black pepper	*Freshly ground black pepper*
For the salad	**For the salad**
1 lb (450g) new potatoes	*1 pound new potatoes*
4 oz (100g) pecan nuts	*1 cup pecan nuts*
1 shallot, chopped	*1 shallot, chopped*
4 large ripe apricots	*4 large ripe apricots*
1 small bunch watercress	*1 small bunch watercress*
1 tablespoon chopped fresh parsley	*1 tablespoon chopped fresh parsley*

1 Place all the ingredients for the dressing into a blender and process until smooth. Set aside.

2 Cook the potatoes until tender, then cut into chunks, peeling if preferred. Place in a large, shallow salad bowl with the nuts and shallot.

3 Plunge the apricots briefly into boiling water, then skin, halve, remove the pit and cut into chunks. Place in the salad bowl.

4 Pour the dressing over the salad and stir gently to amalgamate the ingredients. This should be done while the potatoes are still warm, so that they absorb the flavour. Leave the salad to cool.

5 Trim the stalks from the watercress, wash the leaves and drain well. Arrange the leaves around the edge of the bowl and sprinkle the chopped parsley over the salad. Serve at once.

La Salade Ronsard

ORANGE AND SPINACH SALAD WITH ROQUEFORT DRESSING
Serves 4

Pierre Ronsard was the youngest son of the Maitre d'Hotel du Roi Francis I. The 'Prince of Poets', as his generation called him, wrote a poem called *La Salade* in which he used this choice of food as a model for the simple life, contrasting the natural healthfulness of country life with the pomp and artifice of the Court.

Imperial (Metric)	American
For the dressing	**For the dressing**
2 tablespoons rosé wine	2 tablespoons rosé wine
2 tablespoons walnut oil	2 tablespoons walnut oil
Juice and grated rind of 1 orange	Juice and grated rind of 1 orange
2 oz (50g) crumbled Roquefort	½ cup crumbled Roquefort
1 tablespoon chopped fresh chervil	1 tablespoon chopped fresh chervil
Sea salt	Sea salt
Freshly ground black pepper	Freshly ground black pepper
For the salad	**For the salad**
6 thick slices bread	6 thick slices bread
1 clove garlic	1 clove garlic
Oil for frying	Oil for frying
1 lb (450g) young spinach leaves	1 pound young spinach leaves
3 oranges, peeled and segmented	3 oranges, peeled and segmented
4 oz (100g) mushrooms, sliced	2 cups sliced mushrooms

1 Place all the ingredients for the dressing into a blender goblet and blend until smooth. Set aside.
2 Remove the crust from the slices of bread, then cut the slices into cubes. Flatten the garlic roughly with the side of a heavy knife.
3 Pour oil into a sauté pan to a depth of about ½ inch (1cm), add the garlic and heat gently. When the garlic is sizzling, add the cubes of bread, a few at a time, and fry until golden, tossing the pan so that the cubes cook evenly. Remove with a slotted spoon and drain on kitchen paper towels.
4 Tear the spinach roughly, removing any tough stems, and place in a large bowl. Add the orange segments and sliced mushrooms.
5 Toss with a little of the dressing, then scatter the warm croûtons over the salad. Serve with the remaining dressing offered separately.

Variation
Lamb's lettuce, also known as corn salad, or salad burnet could take the place of all or part of the spinach.

Melon en Salade à la Montaigne

MELON AND LIME SALAD

Serves 4

Montaigne said: 'I think it is healthier to eat more slowly and less, and to eat more often . . . I should hate as much as to see a German putting water in his wine or a Frenchman drinking it pure . . . it is bad manners, besides being harmful to health and even to pleasure, to eat greedily as I do. I often bite my tongue in the process.'

On the ceiling beam of his study, Montaigne inscribed the words of his favourite Greek and Roman writers. One such, from Terence – 'I am a man: I consider nothing foreign to me.' – typifies the attitude of this great Frenchman. This simple but exotic salad seems to me to represent his concept of good food.

Imperial (Metric)	American
16 vine leaves	16 grape vine leaves
1 Cantaloup or other scented melon	1 Cantaloup or other scented melon
Juice and grated rind of 1 lime	Juice and grated rind of 1 lime
Juice of 1 extra lime	Juice of 1 extra lime
Juice of 1 lemon	Juice of 1 lemon
1 teaspoon clear honey	1 teaspoon clear honey
1 teaspoon fresh chopped coriander	1 teaspoon fresh chopped coriander
Sea salt	Sea salt
Freshly ground black pepper	Freshly ground black pepper

1 If using fresh vine leaves, blanch in boiling water for 5 minutes, then drain. If using vacuum packed leaves, soak in fresh water for about 30 minutes, then rinse and drain. Lay the leaves on 4 individual plates.

2 Halve the melon, scoop out the seeds and discard, and cut the melon into tiny balls with a special scoop (a parisienne cutter). Place the melon in a bowl and toss with the juices, rind, honey, coriander and seasoning. Leave in the refrigerator to marinate for 1 hour.

3 Spoon the melon salad over the vine leaves and serve. The vine leaves should be eaten as part of the salad – their fresh, lemony taste is a delicious adjunct to the cool melon salad.

La Salade Mary Conil

A WARM SALAD OF MUSHROOMS ON TANGERINES AND LETTUCE

Serves 6

Anyone who can put up with me for forty-five years deserves a special award for bravery and fortitude. I have always been a difficult, cantankerous and exacting man, and no one knows this side of my character better than my dear wife Mary. Many young apprentices, who have since become top chefs around the world, remember me as a demanding teacher – but they learned their skills well, come what may. Still it is my wife who has stayed by my side over the years, and I pay tribute to her now with a dish that she herself was responsible for. It is based upon an inspired creation of hers, made when unexpected guests arrived at our home one Sunday, and proves that we have yet another chef in the Conil household!

Imperial (Metric)	*American*
2 oz (50g) butter	*¼ cup butter*
4 chopped shallots	*4 chopped shallots*
1 lb (450g) mushrooms, sliced	*1 pound mushrooms, sliced*
Sea salt	*Sea salt*
Freshly ground black pepper	*Freshly ground black pepper*
4 fl oz (120ml) double cream	*½ cup heavy cream*
4 eggs, beaten	*4 eggs, beaten*
Juice of 1 lemon	*Juice of 1 lemon*
2 oz (50g) fresh brioche crumbs	*1 cup fresh brioche crumbs*
1 head curly endive	*1 head curly chicory*
2 tangerines, segmented	*2 tangerines, segmented*
2 oz (50g) shelled pistachio nuts	*½ cup shelled pistachio nuts*
Freshly chopped tarragon to garnish	*Freshly chopped tarragon to garnish*

1 Melt the butter in a pan and sauté the shallots until tender. Then stir in the mushrooms, cover and simmer for about 3 minutes. Season, and allow to cool.

2 In a bowl, beat together the cream, eggs and lemon juice. Stir in the mushrooms. Then beat in the crumbs. Check the seasoning.

3 Spoon the mixture into 6 greased ramekins, then place these in a baking dish. Fill with hot water to come half way up the sides of the ramekins.

4 Bake in a preheated oven at 400°F/200°C (Gas Mark 6) for 25 minutes. Remove from the oven and leave to cool slightly.

5 While the mushroom custards are cooling, wash and drain the endive, and separate the leaves. Place on individual plates and sprinkle with tangerine segments and pistachio nuts.

6 Turn the warm custards out onto the salad. As they settle, their juices will mingle with the leaves to form a delicious mixture. Sprinkle with chopped tarragon and serve your warm salad at once.

Variations
The salad leaves can be varied endlessly, as can your choice of nuts. Fresh breadcrumbs can take the place of brioche crumbs. I like sometimes to garnish the salad with edible flower petals instead of tarragon.

La Salade Charles Perrault

A FANTASY SALAD OF AVOCADOS, APRICOTS AND STRAWBERRIES

Serves 4

The fairly tales of Charles Perrault are classics of children's literature, but perhaps the best known of all is the Sleeping Beauty. The castle in which the Princess and the Court slept was supposedly inspired by the château of Ussé in the Loire valley. Anyone who has visited it can understand why – perched above the river Indre, its white turrets and towers in magical contrast to the dark woodlands beyond.

Not far from Ussé is the château of Villandry, famous for quite another reason. Its gardens, recreated in original 16th century style, are quite splendid. Of course, it is the vegetable garden that will interest the cook, missing as it is so much produce that we take for granted today – even the humble potato – since the New World had yet to give up many of its secrets to the European palate.

<table>
<tr><td align="center">

Imperial (Metric)
For the dressing
¼ pint (150ml) natural yogurt
Juice and rind of ½ lemon
Juice and rind of ½ orange
1 tablespoon honey or syrup from preserved ginger

</td><td align="center">

American
For the dressing
⅔ cup plain yogurt
Juice and rind of ½ lemon
Juice and rind of ½ orange
1 tablespoon honey or syrup from candied ginger

</td></tr>
<tr><td align="center">

For the salad
A few leaves of curly endive
2 ripe apricots
8 oz (225g) large ripe strawberries
2 ripe avocados

</td><td align="center">

For the salad
A few leaves of curly chicory
2 ripe apricots
2 cups large ripe strawberries
2 ripe avocados

</td></tr>
</table>

1 Beat together all the dressing ingredients. A little black pepper could be added, if wished. Spoon some dressing onto each of four chilled serving plates.
2 Wash and drain the lettuce leaves well, then arrange prettily on the plate, fanning out, flower-like.
3 Plunge the apricots into boiling water for about 1 minute, then drain and peel off the skin. Halve, stone and cut into segments.
4 Hull the strawberries, then slice.
5 Halve and stone (pit) the avocados. To peel, cut the halves lengthwise to make 4 quarters. The skin can then be pulled gently back off the quarters without waste. Cut each piece in half lengthwise again.
6 Arrange slices of apricot, strawberry and avocado prettily on each plate. Serve immediately, offering the remaining dressing separately.

Illustrated opposite page 64.

CHAPTER FOUR

Les Fruits en Entrées

A Bouquet of Main Courses

The sweet-sour flavour is one which always intrigues the gourmet, and eludes the careless cook. Yet how appetizing it can be when carried out successfully. And the balance of savoury and sweet, different yet linked in its appeal to the palate, is a taste worth pursuing.

Every nation has its specialities in this area – in India the sambal is a sweet-sharp complement to dishes which in themselves often balance the savoury with the natural sweetness of fruit; the Orient is most commonly associated with a perfect balance of these two contrasting elements; America offers both Northern savoury pancakes with a garnish of maple syrup, and the Southern Creole treats of pulse and fruit combinations; the British appreciate the sharp tang of gooseberry, redcurrant and apple with traditional fare; and we French have always understood the virtues of a piquant sauce of citrus to cut the richness of a classic dish.

Variety is the key. The human palate seems to seek out such contrasts in a single dish. Just as a counterpoint of hot and cold is pleasing to us (from childhood, when ice-cream with a hot chocolate sauce is luxury indeed), so a savoury dish which is augmented with a fruity element seems to fire the appetite in a special way.

It is easy to see how the boundaries between sweet and savoury are blurred. Take, for example, the classic French *clafoutis*. This simple country dish is based upon fruit cooked with a sweet batter – not so dissimilar to the English Toad in the Hole or Yorkshire Pudding. How easy, then, to add a savoury element to the batter, by the removal of sugar and the addition of herbs, cheese or whatever your palate should prefer, and to retain the fruity ingredients. Why, in the past, mincemeat such as Dickens ate contained just what its name suggests; similarly those very Yorkshire puddings often had more than a taste of dried peel, currants or whatever the thrifty cook had stored up for Winter use.

Today we often take such contrasts for

granted, without thinking twice about this natural combination. I have already mentioned the sort of fruit sauce that naturally accompanies the family 'roast'. The stuffing, too, usually has a fruity element. Why should such combinations be confined to carnivores? Surely the healthy diet is even more attuned to the appreciation of the subtle marriage of fruit, vegetable and pulse or grain?

In this chapter you will find many variations of this happy balance, and the choices open to you, the cook, in this respect, are endless. The harvests of the fields and orchards have always lent themselves to flexibility – you can make your own choice of flavours in so many of the recipes that follow, that you have in the next few pages a magic carpet of ideas upon which to float your own preferences and local bounty!

Clafoutis de Brugnons au Petit Lait

BAKED NECTARINES IN A CHEESY BUTTERMILK BATTER

Serves 4

Nectarines are the result of a cross between the peach and the plum. They have the skin of a plum, the stone of a peach, and the flavour of both. This natural mutation originated in China and came to the Western world via Persia. Now they are widely grown and appreciated. Here I have chosen to cloak them in a savoury version of the traditional French baked *clafoutis* batter. Crusty bread and a simple salad are all that is required to make a splendid luncheon dish.

Imperial (Metric)	*American*
4 eggs	*4 eggs*
1 teaspoon sea salt	*1 teaspoon sea salt*
3 oz (75g) wholemeal flour	*¾ cup whole wheat flour*
12 fl oz (350ml) buttermilk	*1½ cups buttermilk*
½ teaspoon mixed spice	*½ teaspoon mixed spice*
Freshly ground black pepper	*Freshly ground black pepper*
2 oz (50g) butter	*¼ cup butter*
4 nectarines	*4 nectarines*
1 tablespoon rum or cognac	*1 tablespoon rum or cognac*
2 oz (50g) grated cheese	*½ cup grated cheese*

1 Beat the eggs with the salt for 4 minutes. Then beat in the flour until well mixed. Gradually beat in the buttermilk, then stir in the spice and season with black pepper.
2 Grease a large earthenware baking dish with the butter.
3 Halve and stone the nectarines; lay them in the base of the baking dish, cut sides upward. Sprinkle with the rum or cognac.
4 Pour the batter over the nectarines, sprinkle with cheese, then place the dish in a preheated oven at 350°F/180°C (Gas Mark 4) and bake for 45 minutes, or until the batter is risen and set. Serve hot or at room temperature.

Flan de Citrouille au Fromage

PUMPKIN AND POTATO BAKE WITH GRAPES AND CHEESE

Serves 4

In France, we have two different words for pumpkin, which distinguish two quite different types. First, there is *potiron*, which is smooth-skinned and can grow to a quite formidable size. Its orange flesh is at its most fruity at around the 4 to 8 kilo size. Then there is the *citrouille* with paler flesh and a ribbed outer skin. Étampes in France is famed for its sweet, red-fleshed pumpkin, and in Boulogne I have seen a huge, grey-fleshed variety.

I have used *citrouille* in this recipe, but it will taste just as good made with whichever variety of this versatile fruit is available to you.

Imperial (Metric)	*American*
2 lb (1 kilo) pumpkin flesh	*2 pounds pumpkin flesh*
8 oz (225g) potatoes	*½ pound potatoes*
4 oz (100g) butter	*½ cup butter*
Sea salt	*Sea salt*
Freshly ground black pepper	*Freshly ground black pepper*
1 teaspoon honey	*1 teaspoon honey*
Juice and grated rind of 2 lemons	*Juice and grated rind of 2 lemons*
4 eggs	*4 eggs*
3 oz (75g) Brie cheese	*¾ cup Brie cheese*
2 oz (50g) seedless green grapes	*1 cup seedless green grapes*
3 oz (75g) grated Gruyère cheese	*¾ cup grated Gruyère cheese*
2 oz (50g) wholemeal breadcrumbs	*1 cup whole wheat breadcrumbs*

1 Cut the pumpkin flesh into rough chunks. Scrub and dice the potatoes. Boil together in plenty of salted water for 25 minutes, or until tender. Drain well and then mash until smooth.

2 Beat half the butter into the pumpkin purée, then season and stir in the honey and lemon.

3 Beat the eggs and add to the mixture, stirring until well mixed.

4 Cut the Brie into small dice, then stir these and the grapes into the mixture.

5 Use a little of the remaining butter to grease an earthenware dish, then fill with the pumpkin mixture, smoothing the top with a palette knife.

6 Mix together the breadcrumbs and Gruyère. Sprinkle over the dish. Dot with the remaining butter.

7 Place the dish in a preheated oven at 400°F/200°C (Gas Mark 6) and cook until warmed through and brown and sizzling on top, then serve.

Opposite Fantasy Salad of Avocado, Apricots and Strawberries (page 60).

Potiron à la Provençale

PUMPKIN RISOTTO

Serves 4

Here is our second pumpkin supper dish – this time a fragrant rice dish, redolent with the garlic aromas of Southern France from whence it comes.

Imperial (Metric)	American
3 lb (1.5 kilos) pumpkin	3 pound pumpkin
1 large red onion	1 large red onion
4 oz (100g) butter	½ cup butter
4 cloves garlic, crushed	4 cloves garlic, crushed
4 oz (100g) brown rice	½ cup brown rice
1 pint (600ml) vegetable stock	2½ cups vegetable stock
1 bouquet garni	1 bouquet garni
2 oz (50g) sultanas	⅓ cup golden seedless raisins
1 oz (25g) flaked almonds	¼ cup slivered almonds
1 tablespoon chopped parsley	1 tablespoon chopped parsley

1 Remove the skin and seeds from the pumpkin and chop into ½ inch (1cm) chunks. Peel and chop the onion.

2 Heat the butter in a metal casserole and gently sauté the onion and garlic until tender. Then add the rice and cook, stirring, so that the fat impregnates the grains.

3 Add the stock to the pan, then stir in the pumpkin and bouquet garni. Stir well, cover, and place in a preheated oven at 400°F/200°C (Gas Mark 6). Cook for about 35 minutes, or until the rice is cooked and the liquid absorbed. About 5 minutes before the end of the cooking time, stir in the sultanas (raisins).

4 Remove the casserole from the oven, discard the bouquet garni, check the seasoning. Sprinkle with the almonds and parsley and serve with a simple tomato salad.

Opposite Savoury Fruited Rice (page 69).

Les Petits Flans de Tomates aux Olives Bordelaise

LITTLE TOMATO AND OLIVE FLANS

Serves 4

I should begin by saying that the term flan does not necessarily imply a pastry case. These little custards, baked in the oven, are encased only in ramekin dishes, although they could adapt to the traditional pastry mould if you preferred.

In Bordeaux there is a record of a Hôtellerie of 1650 known as *Des Trois Conils*. It was famed for its food, and also for its best customers, the Conils, who served in a regiment of Musketeers. Their ribald drinking bouts were the talk of the town. Today, an ancient street in that fair city still recalls them – *La Rue des Trois Conils*.

Imperial (Metric)	American
2 oz (50g) butter	¼ cup butter
3 large eggs	3 large eggs
8 oz (225g) cream cheese	1 cup cream cheese
½ pint (300ml) natural yogurt	1⅓ cups plain yogurt
Sea salt	Sea salt
Freshly ground black pepper	Freshly ground black pepper
8 oz (225g) tomatoes, skinned, seeded and chopped	1½ cups skinned, seeded and chopped tomatoes
4 oz (100g) corn kernels	⅔ cup corn kernels
6 olives, stoned and chopped	6 olives, pitted and chopped
1 tablespoon fresh chopped mint	1 tablespoon fresh chopped mint

1 Grease four metal pudding moulds or ramekins with the butter.
2 Beat together the eggs, cheese and yogurt. Season well.
3 Into the egg mixture, stir the tomatoes, corn, olives and mint. Spoon this into the ramekins, then place the dishes in a deep tray. Fill to half way up the sides of the dishes with hot water.
4 Place the tray on the centre shelf of a preheated oven at 400°F/200°C (Gas Mark 6) and bake for 35 to 40 minutes, or until the custards are set.
5 To serve, arrange a few leaves of curly lettuce on four individual plates. Leave the custards to stand for a few minutes before turning out onto the leaves, then serve at once.

Gratinées des Causses

ONION AND BLUE CHEESE CASSEROLE WITH PRUNES AND WALNUTS

Serves 4

The Causses region of France is wild and rocky, and its people depend on the produce from its goats and sheep for much of their nourishment. Of course, the most famous product of all is Roquefort cheese, which is famed throughout the world. This dish uses just a little of that fabulous cheese, yet its flavour is intense and good. A simple dish, it may look at first more like a soup than a casserole, but it is substantial and rich in nutrients. In the Winter, served with good bread, it's all that's needed to take the chill from your bones.

Imperial (Metric)	American
4 oz (100g) butter	½ cup butter
1 lb (450g) onions, sliced	1 pound onions, sliced
3 pints (1.7 litres) vegetable stock	7½ cups vegetable stock
4 oz (100g) Roquefort cheese	½ cup Roquefort cheese
3 fl oz (90ml) Cognac	⅓ cup Cognac
2 egg yolks	2 egg yolks
Sea salt	Sea salt
Freshly ground black pepper	Freshly ground black pepper
4 slices French bread	4 slices French bread
4 oz (100g) chopped walnuts	1 cup chopped walnuts
8 prunes, stoned and soaked	8 prunes, pitted and soaked
4 oz (100g) grated Cantal cheese	1 cup grated Cantal cheese

1 Melt half the butter in a large *marmite* or flameproof casserole. Add the onions and sauté gently until golden and soft. Pour in the stock and boil for 15 minutes.
2 Meanwhile, cream together the butter, Roquefort and brandy. Beat in 4 tablespoons of stock to form a smooth paste, then add the egg yolks and beat again.
3 Remove the casserole from the heat and gradually add the cheese cream, stirring well to mix. Reheat gently until the stew is thick and creamy.
4 Toast the bread and set aside.
5 In 4 individual bowls, place an equal amount of nuts and prunes, then pour the creamy onion mixture over each.
6 Lay a slice of toast on each bowl, sprinkle with grated cheese and brown under a hot grill (broiler) until sizzling and piping hot. Serve at once.

Croustillant des Clos

CHEESE AND CIDER APPLE PUDDINGS

Serves 4

It is amazing what family treasures are unearthed that, at the time, had little significance. One brother of my great-grandmother was quite an artist, and won a prize for his paintings in Rome. This coveted award was treated with low esteem by a family of chefs, with the exception that his self-portrait once graced our dining room. Yet, as part of the fashionable scene of Paris he befriended many great artists, including Chopin and Georges Sand, and this recipe was served by him at one of the exclusive parties he gave. Fine cookery is indeed the prerogative of the artist, and art will always be dear to the chef.

Imperial (Metric)	*American*
4 teaspoons oil	*4 teaspoons oil*
2 large eggs	*2 large eggs*
½ pint (300ml) buttermilk	*1⅓ cups buttermilk*
Sea salt	*Sea salt*
Freshly ground black pepper	*Freshly ground black pepper*
1 tablespoon Calvados	*1 tablespoon Calvados*
4 oz (100g) wholemeal bread flour	*1 cup whole wheat bread flour*
1 large cider apple	*1 large cider apple*
4 oz (100g) grated Gruyère cheese	*1 cup grated Gruyère cheese*

1 Oil 4 metal dariole moulds (2 inches/5cm deep and 1½ inches/4cm in diameter). Place the moulds in a metal baking tray.

2 Beat together the eggs and buttermilk. Season well, then stir in the Calvados. Gradually sift in the flour, beating well between each addition.

3 Place the moulds in a hot oven at 425°F/225°C (Gas Mark 7) for 5 minutes. Then remove and half-fill each with batter. Return to the oven for 5 minutes more.

4 Meanwhile, peel, core and slice the apple. Remove the moulds from the oven and divide the apple between them, pressing gently into the mould. Top up with the remaining batter and return to the oven for about 20 minutes.

5 When the puddings are well-risen and golden, about 5 minutes before the end of cooking, sprinkle each with cheese and continue the cooking, so that the cheese melts and forms a delicious crust.

6 Serve hot with a glass of good French cider.

Riz aux Fruits d'Andalousie à la Conil

SAVOURY FRUITED RICE

Serves 4

The town of Conil in Spain was founded by Guzman in 1407. He was one of the many illegitimate sons of Alphonso, King of Aragon and Castille. He was also one of the first recorded to be given the title bearing our name, and it is from he that we are descended. My line emigrated to France in the fifteenth century. This dish is for my grandchildren, Philip, Matthew and Nicole – I have pictures of them standing in the sunshine by the sign that announces the home town of their forefathers.

Imperial (Metric)	American
8 oz (225g) brown rice	2 cups brown rice
3 fl oz (90ml) olive oil	⅓ cup olive oil
Juice of 1 orange	Juice of 1 orange
Juice of 1 lemon	Juice of 1 lemon
Sea salt	Sea salt
Freshly ground black pepper	Freshly ground black pepper
½ teaspoon mixed spices	½ teaspoon mixed spices
2 large tomatoes, skinned, seeded and chopped	2 large tomatoes, skinned, seeded and chopped
3 oz (75g) seedless raisins	½ cup seedless raisins
2 ripe apricots, skinned, stoned and chopped	2 ripe apricots, skinned, pitted and chopped
2 spring onions, chopped	2 scallions, chopped
8 stuffed olives, sliced	8 stuffed olives, sliced
1 tablespoon chopped parsley	1 tablespoon chopped parsley
1 tablespoon chopped mint	1 tablespoon chopped mint
2 hard boiled eggs, chopped	2 hard cooked eggs, chopped

1 Boil the rice until tender, then drain and place in a large bowl.

2 Beat together the oil, fruit juices, seasoning and spices. Toss with the hot rice.

3 Stir in the tomatoes, raisins, apricots, spring onions (scallions) and olives, then sprinkle with the herbs and chopped egg. Serve at once. This dish is equally good served cold. A glass of Southern French red wine is good with the hot dish, or chilled Manzanilla sherry with the cold version.

Illustrated opposite page 65.

Les Feuilletés de Fromage de Chèvre aux Reines Claudes

GOAT'S CHEESE CUSHIONS WITH GREENGAGE SAUCE

Serves 6

The centre of these light puff pastry parcels is filled with a luscious mixture of goat's cheese, garlic, pine kernels and basil, and the finished dish is transformed into pure heaven by a simple sauce of that evocative fruit, the greengage. Quintessentially French, the heady power of the greengage is captured most atmospherically by the author Rumer Godden, in her novel *The Greengage Summer*, set in Château Thierry in Northern France. The piquant bitter-sweet of adolescence is counterpointed by the lush ripeness of a summer orchard of greengages on the banks of the Marne.

Imperial (Metric)	*American*
For the parcels	**For the parcels**
6 oz (175g) fresh Chèvre	*¾ cup fresh Chèvre*
1 clove garlic, crushed	*1 clove garlic, crushed*
1 tablespoon fresh chopped basil	*1 tablespoon fresh chopped basil*
1 tablespoon chopped pine kernels	*1 tablespoon chopped pine kernels*
Sea salt	*Sea salt*
Freshly ground black pepper	*Freshly ground black pepper*
12 oz (350g) packet wholemeal puff pastry	*¾ pound pack whole wheat puff pastry*
Beaten egg to glaze	*Beaten egg to glaze*
For the sauce	**For the sauce**
12 oz (350g) ripe greengages	*¾ pound ripe greengages*
2 tablespoons redcurrant jelly	*2 tablespoons redcurrant jelly*
2 tablespoons Armagnac	*2 tablespoons Armagnac*
To serve	**To serve**
3 fl oz (90ml) double cream, warmed	*⅓ cup heavy cream, warmed*
Fresh basil sprigs	*Fresh basil sprigs*

1 Mash together the goat's cheese, garlic, basil and pine kernels. Taste (the goat's cheese may be salty) and season accordingly.

2 Roll out the pastry quite thinly. Cut out 13 circles or heart-shapes about 3 inches (7.5cm) in diameter. Line 6 patty tins with pastry. Brush the edges of each with beaten egg.

3 Divide the cheese mixture between the pastry shells, then top with the remaining pastry shapes and pinch the edges to seal well. Glaze with beaten egg.

4 Bake at 400°F/200°C (Gas Mark 6) for 15 to 20 minutes, until puffed and golden.

5 Meanwhile, make the sauce. Halve, skin and pit the greengages. Place the flesh in a blender with the redcurrant jelly and Armagnac, and purée until smooth.

6 Spoon a little of the sauce onto six serving plates and serve a cheese cushion straight from the oven onto them. Make a little hole in the top of each and pour in a spoonful of warm cream. Garnish with sprigs of basil and serve at once, with a side salad of bitter salad leaves.

Oeufs en Cocotte Maximilienne

BAKED EGGS WITH AVOCADO AND TOMATO

Serves 4

These rich little pots make an unusual supper dish, served with crusty French bread, or could form the appetizer to a light main course. This dish is named for the Emperor Maximilien, enthroned by Napoléon III as the ruling sovereign of Mexico. Thousands of Frenchmen died to support his regime, and the French government paid a huge ransom to support it. Nevertheless, Mexico remained a friendly nation, and aspects of her spicy cuisine came to be mingled with traditional French styles. This dish reflects that – a spicy avocado and tomato mixture topped by a classic French method of cooking eggs.

Imperial (Metric)	American
2 oz (50g) butter	¼ cup butter
2 tablespoons olive oil	2 tablespoons olive oil
2 shallots, chopped	2 shallots, chopped
1 clove garlic, crushed	1 clove garlic, crushed
Chopped flesh of 1 ripe avocado	Chopped flesh of 1 ripe avocado
2 tomatoes, skinned, seeded and chopped	2 tomatoes, skinned, seeded and chopped
Dash of Tabasco	Dash of Tabasco
Sea salt	Sea salt
Freshly ground black pepper	Freshly ground black pepper
4 large eggs	4 large eggs
4 teaspoons buttermilk	4 teaspoons buttermilk
4 sprigs fresh coriander	4 sprigs fresh coriander

1 Use half the butter to grease four largish ramekins.

2 Heat the remaining butter with the oil in a pan. Sauté the shallots and garlic until just soft, then stir in the avocado and tomatoes and cook for 30 seconds only. Add Tabasco and seasoning to taste, then divide the mixture between the ramekins.

3 Break an egg into each ramekin, then place them in a deep metal tray and fill with hot water to half-way up the ramekins. Bake at 425°F/220°C (Gas Mark 7) for 7 to 10 minutes, or until the eggs are just set but not hard.

4 Remove from the oven and spoon a little buttermilk over each. Decorate with coriander, chopped if wished, and serve at once.

Fricassée de Choux à l'Ananas

SPICY CABBAGE FRICASSEE WITH PINEAPPLE

Serves 4

Pineapple has an affinity with cabbage, both in flavour and texture, and contributes greatly to the overall effect of this quick and easy dish, which is almost like a hot coleslaw but with a different and far more subtle and elusive taste. For best effect, you need a really fresh Savoy cabbage and fresh pineapple.

Imperial (Metric)	American
2 oz (50g) butter	¼ cup butter
1 large onion, sliced	1 large onion, sliced
2 cloves garlic, finely chopped	2 cloves garlic, finely chopped
1 small Savoy cabbage, cored and shredded	1 small Savoy cabbage, cored and shredded
½ red pepper, seeded and sliced	½ red pepper, seeded and sliced
1 small piece ginger	1 small piece ginger
2 fl oz (60ml) pineapple juice	¼ cup pineapple juice
½ pint (300ml) water	1⅓ cups water
1 tablespoon soy sauce	1 tablespoon soy sauce
Sea salt	Sea salt
Freshly ground black pepper	Freshly ground black pepper
6 oz (175g) fresh pineapple, cubed	1 cup fresh pineapple, cubed
4 oz (100g) cashew nuts	1 cup cashew nuts
¼ pint (150ml) natural yogurt	⅔ cup plain yogurt

1 Heat the butter in a large pan and sauté the onion and garlic for 2 minutes. Then stir in the cabbage and pepper and cook gently for a further 3 minutes.
2 In a blender, purée together the ginger and pineapple juice, then stir this into the cabbage. Add the water and soy sauce, cover and simmer for 6 minutes. Season to taste.
3 Once the cabbage has softened, add the pineapple and nuts and heat through.
4 Just before serving, stir in the yogurt and heat through but do not boil. Serve with new or baked potatoes.

Les Tomates au Roquefort et aux Noix

TOMATOES STUFFED WITH A ROQUEFORT AND WALNUT SOUFFLÉ

Serves 4

The large, ribbed tomatoes are my favourites for holding a savoury filling, but it is wise to sample one before embarking on a dish for a special occasion, as they have been known to be disappointingly watery now and again. When good, however, they can be used for a multitude of dishes – lightly poached vegetables in mayonnaise; pasta or rice salad; a savoury bake of flavoured vegetables, breadcrumbs and/or rice . . . what fun to invent a tasty morsel to fill this little cup which itself is good to eat! This filling is one of my best-loved. It is a cross between scrambled and souffléd eggs, flavoured with piquant cheese and given texture with niblets of walnut. Two tomatoes each makes a satisfying main course for even the most hungry diner, or a single tomato could be paired with another stuffed vegetable, or offered as an appetizer on its own, or form part of a buffet, or accompany another sort of main course dish. You can choose!

Imperial (Metric)	*American*
8 large tomatoes	*8 large tomatoes*

For the scramble	**For the scramble**
2 oz (50g) crumbled Roquefort	*½ cup crumbled Roquefort*
2 oz (50g) crushed walnuts	*½ cup crushed walnuts*
4 leaves basil, shredded	*4 leaves basil, shredded*
2 oz (50g) butter	*¼ cup butter*
1 whole egg	*1 whole egg*
2 egg yolks	*2 egg yolks*
Freshly ground black pepper	*Freshly ground black pepper*

For the soufflé	**For the soufflé**
1 oz (25g) butter	*2 tablespoons butter*
1 oz (25g) flour	*¼ cup flour*
3 fl oz (90ml) buttermilk	*⅓ cup buttermilk*
2 fl oz (60ml) water	*¼ cup water*
3 egg yolks	*3 egg yolks*
5 egg whites	*5 egg whites*
Pinch sea salt	*Pinch sea salt*

1 Slice off the base of each tomato, opposite the eye, one-third of the way down. Scoop out the pulp from each and reserve for use in another dish. Set the tomatoes, cut side down, in a dish to drain off excess juices.

2 For the scramble mixture, pass the cheese through a sieve (strainer) into a bowl, then beat in the nuts and basil. Heat the butter in a pan and add the cheese mixture to melt slightly.

3 Beat the first batch of eggs together and add to the pan. Scramble gently until barely cooked, season with pepper then transfer to a bowl.

4 For the soufflé mix, heat the rest of the butter in a clean pan, then add the flour and cook to form a roux. Gradually add the liquids and stir until a thick, smooth sauce is obtained.

5 Add the cheese and walnut mixture to the sauce and stir well to blend. Remove from the heat.

6 Beat the egg whites with a pinch of salt and fold half into the scramble mixture, then gradually fold in the rest.

7 Place the tomatoes in the indentations of a cake (patty) tin to hold them in position. Fill each tomato with the mixture.

8 Place the pan in a preheated oven at 375°F/190°C (Gas Mark 5) for about 20 minutes, or until the soufflé is risen and golden. Serve at once.

Le Banania des Antilles

VEGETABLE STEW WITH BANANA AND RUM

Serves 4

Creole cuisine is a mixture of the most imaginative of both African and French cookery. Spicy and exotic flavours are at the forefront, reflecting the use of unusual ingredients, especially tropical fruits. This simple stew could be made with any of the 'new' produce coming into our food markets from the Caribbean – chayote, christophene, breadfruit, plantain . . . be adventurous, and take your pick.

Imperial (Metric)	*American*
3 fl oz (90ml) coconut oil	*⅓ cup coconut oil*
1 large onion, chopped	*1 large onion, chopped*
3 cloves garlic, crushed	*3 cloves garlic, crushed*
1 teaspoon curry powder	*1 teaspoon curry powder*
2 tablespoons tomato purée	*2 tablespoons tomato paste*
½ pint (300ml) coconut milk	*1⅓ cups coconut milk*
1 chilli, seeded and finely sliced	*1 chili, seeded and finely sliced*
1 chayote, peeled and chopped	*1 chayote, peeled and chopped*
1 mango, peeled and chopped	*1 mango, peeled and chopped*
1 plantain or 2 unripe bananas, peeled and sliced	*1 plantain or 2 unripe bananas, peeled and sliced*
Sea salt	*Sea salt*
Freshly ground black pepper	*Freshly ground black pepper*
2 tablespoons white rum	*2 tablespoons white rum*
Juice of 1 lime	*Juice of 1 lime*

1 Heat the oil in a large, lidded pan, and sauté the onion and garlic for 2 minutes without browning. Add the curry powder and continue cooking for a further minute. Then stir in the tomato purée (paste), followed by the coconut milk. Stir well to blend everything.
2 Add the chilli, chayote, mango and plantain or banana to the pan. Bring to a boil, cover, turn down the heat and simmer for 25 minutes, or until all the ingredients are tender.
3 Season to taste and stir in the rum and lime juice. Serve accompanied by rice or beans.

Note
If chayote is unavailable, you could substitute another exotic vegetable fruit. If nothing comes to hand, unpeeled, sliced courgettes (about 8 ounces/225g) make a pleasant alternative.

Le Couscous aux Fruits

GOLDEN, FRUITED COUSCOUS

Serves 4

The evocation of Africa is strong in this dish from the southern coast of France, yet it can be made with whatever simple fruits and vegetables are available to you. Couscous is invaluable to the cook in a hurry, or the cook on a budget, yet you can also lavish as much time and money as you care to on making it into a very special supper dish for family meals or for entertaining friends. This flexible dish is surely most representative of the pleasures of inventive cooking.

Imperial (Metric)	*American*
2 pints (1.1 litres) good vegetable stock	*5 cups good vegetable stock*
9 oz (275g) couscous	*1½ cups couscous*
2 oz (50g) butter	*¼ cup vegetable stock*
1 onion, chopped	*1 onion, chopped*
4 oz (115g) diced vegetables	*1 cup diced vegetables*
1 oz (25g) each dried apricots, dates, apples, sultanas	*⅓ cup each dried apricots, dates, apples, golden raisins*
¼ pint (150ml) fruit juice	*⅓ cup fruit juice*
Sea salt	*Sea salt*
Freshly ground black pepper	*Freshly ground black pepper*
1 teaspoon ground cumin	*1 teaspoon ground cumin*
Good pinch turmeric	*Good pinch turmeric*
Toasted flaked almonds	*Toasted slivered almonds*

1 Heat the stock to boiling. Place the couscous in a bowl and pour on two-thirds of the boiling stock. Set aside for 10 minutes to soak.

2 In a large pan, heat the butter and sauté the onion and vegetables for 2 minutes. Add the couscous and the remaining stock, cover and cook for 5 minutes, stirring once or twice.

3 Meanwhile, soak the fruit in the juice. When the couscous has been cooking for 5 minutes, add the soaked fruit to the pan. Season to taste and add the spices. Stir well.

4 Turn the contents of the pan into an earthenware dish and cover. Place in a preheated oven at 400°F/200°C (Gas Mark 6) for 10 minutes. Just before serving, sprinkle with almonds, allow to heat through then serve.

CHAPTER FIVE

Les Entremets Froids

Chilled Fruit Desserts from the Dairy

There is something especially luxurious and satisfying about a creamy fruit combination, served chilled, in small portions, at the end of a meal. But the fact that a dessert includes cream, eggs or yogurt does not mean that it has to be rich, heavy or stodgy. Indeed, the very fact that this produce is counterpointed with piquant fruit means that a lightness of flavour will be added to the finished dish.

Normandy is the region of France most often identified with the goodness of the dairy – its green pastures are the home of mild-faced cattle that produce milk of an exceptional quality. From that comes the rich cream, butter and famed cheeses of the region. Yogurt is relatively new in French cooking, and there are purists who will argue that it has no place there, but anyone who values their health and prefers to keep a

freshness in their palate throughout a good meal will appreciate its contribution to the newer styles of cooking. Now that high quality low-fat varieties can be found it can take its place with the lower-fat curd cheeses as an asset to any cook's list of ingredients.

The apple is Normandy's main fruit, and its influence extends to the fine cider and noble apple brandy Calvados, which merits a place alongside Cognac and Armagnac as one of the great distilled drinks of France. But fruits of all sorts, both native to France and from more unusual and exotic climes, are to be found within the following pages. They serve to balance the dairy produce, adding a fresh, natural sweetness with just the right touch of sharpness to round off the meal in satisfying style.

Le Sorbet aux Brugnons

NECTARINE AND CHABLIS ICE

Serves 4

We last encountered nectarines blanketed in a cheesy buttermilk batter. Here they are disguised yet again, this time puréed in a delicate sorbet with good French wine and natural yogurt. I have chosen to use Chablis, which is perfect for a special occasion – dry yet mellow enough to give a full flavour to the dish. However, any dry white wine with a suitable depth will suffice to replace it, and you can save your *premier crû* to drink with the meal.

Imperial (Metric)	American
4 large, ripe nectarines	4 large, ripe nectarines
¾ pint (450ml) water	2 cups water
¼ pint (150ml) Chablis	⅔ cup Chablis
6 oz (175g) sugar	1 cup sugar
¼ pint (150ml) natural yogurt	⅔ cup plain yogurt
2 egg whites	2 egg whites

1 Stone the nectarines, cut into pieces, place the nectarine flesh in a pan with the water and cook until tender. Purée in a blender until smooth.
2 Return the purée to the pan, add the wine and sugar, and cook, stirring, until the sugar is dissolved. Boil for 2 to 3 minutes.
3 Cool slightly before stirring in the yogurt, then pour into a freezer tray. Freeze until slushy.
4 Whisk the egg whites until stiff but not 'dry'. Fold lightly into the semi-frozen sorbet. Return to the freezer and freeze until firm. (Or follow this procedure according to the instructions of an ice-cream machine.)
5 Serve scoops of sorbet on pools of cream that has been flavoured with a dash of Cointreau whipped in, and garnish with parings of orange peel.

Illustrated opposite page 96.

Le Melon Glacé Népal

MELON AND PEACH SHERBET

Serves 4

In the Summer of 1937 I was working at the Hermitage Hotel, Le Touquet. One day, whilst taking a well-earned break on the sands, I saw an English nanny remonstrating with her little charge for hitting one of his French playmates on the head with a spade. Later, at a children's party at the hotel, I was to discover that the mischievous young aggressor was the future King of Nepal. Well, all small children are alike in good and naughty behaviour after all! We served this sherbet then, and all the children were as good as gold.

This dish is a cross between a water ice and the now-fashionable frozen yogurt.

Imperial (Metric)	*American*
1 medium Cantaloup orange-fleshed melon	*1 medium Cantaloup orange-fleshed melon*
2 ripe peaches	*2 ripe peaches*
1 tablespoon blanched almonds	*1 tablespoon blanched almonds*
6 oz (150g) sugar	*1 cup sugar*
¼ pint (150ml) natural yogurt	*⅔ cup plain yogurt*
2 egg whites	*2 egg whites*
Slices of peach, to decorate	*Slices of peach, to decorate*
Melon balls, to decorate	*Melon balls, to decorate*

1 Halve the melon; scoop out the seeds and discard. Scoop the fruit into a blender or food processor.

2 Skin, halve and pit the peaches. Chop the fruit and add it to the melon flesh.

3 Add the almonds, then purée the mixture until smooth.

4 Spoon the purée into a shallow container, then stir in the sugar and yogurt. Freeze until 'slushy'.

5 Beat the egg whites until stiff, but not 'dry', and fold them into the semi-frozen sorbet.

6 Return to the freezer until firm. The sherbet should be removed ahead of serving, to return to a slightly softened state. Spoon into tall, stemmed glasses and decorate with peach and melon, then serve at once.

Crème d'Annone

FROZEN CUSTARD APPLE CREAM

Serves 4

The flavour of this wonderful exotic fruit is a cross between that of pineapple and banana, and its consistency is that of custard – hence its name. It can be used for a variety of desserts and drinks, by simply puréeing it with other ingredients, such as cream, liqueurs and so forth. Still relatively new to most countries, but now more commonly imported than it once was, it is well worth seeking out if you wish to try a new experience in flavour. Here is a simple introduction to this exciting fruit.

Imperial (Metric)	*American*
2 egg whites	*2 egg whites*
4 oz (100g) caster sugar	*⅔ cup superfine sugar*
2 ripe custard apples	*2 ripe custard apples*
Juice of ½ lemon	*Juice of ½ lemon*
2 tablespoons double cream	*2 tablespoons double cream*

1 In a double boiler over barely simmering water, beat the egg whites until fluffy. Then beat in the sugar and continue to whisk until the mixture resembles lightly whipped cream. Remove from the heat and set aside to cool.

2 Halve and seed the custard apples. Mash the flesh in a bowl with the lemon juice and cream.

3 Fold the egg whites into the fruit cream and transfer to a freezer container.

4 When the mixture is half-frozen, remove and beat well. Return to the freezer until completely frozen. Remove from the freezer for 20 minutes before serving.

Neige de Rhubarbe aux Framboises

RHUBARB SNOW WITH RASPBERRIES

Serves 4

Rhubarb is, in fact, a vegetable – in the past, its leaves were used like spinach – and yet it can be used to make a whole host of delicious desserts. However, rhubarb leaves contain oxalic acid, which can be harmful. It is a perfect base for a light dish such as this, its subtle flavour paired with aromatic fresh raspberries. We have chosen to use a liquid sweetener in this dish, making it a perfect dessert for diabetics and dieters alike, as well as for anyone who wants to finish a meal in style without feeling over-full.

Imperial (Metric)	American
1 lb (450g) rhubarb	1 pound rhubarb
1 tea bag	1 tea bag
6 oz (150g) raspberries	1 cup raspberries
4 fl oz (120ml) natural yogurt	½ cup plain yogurt
4 oz (115g) cottage cheese	½ cup farmer's cheese
12 drops liquid sweetener	12 drops liquid sweetener
2 egg whites	2 egg whites
Pinch sea salt	Pinch sea salt

1 Wash, trim and cut the rhubarb into chunks. Place in a pan of water, bring to the boil and cook until tender. Remove from the heat and add the tea bag. Leave to cool, removing the tea bag after 5 minutes.

2 When cool, drain the rhubarb and place in a blender or food processor. Clean the raspberries and add half to the rhubarb. Blend to a purée.

3 Place the mixture in a bowl and beat in the yogurt and cheese. Stir in the sweetener to taste.

4 Beat the egg whites with a pinch of salt, until stiff. Fold them into the fruit mixture, then pour into tall glasses. Decorate with the remaining raspberries and serve at once.

Gelée de Vin de Provence aux Mirabelles
ROSÉ WINE AND WHITE PLUM JELLY

Serves 4

This delicate sweet jelly uses agar-agar as a gelling agent – it is quite as good as gelatine, and doesn't rely upon bones and hooves for its setting qualities, since it is derived from seaweed. Very little sugar is needed for this dish. The wine, and the natural sweetness of the fruit, gives the jelly most of the sweetness it needs.

Mirabelles are tiny golden-white plums, about the size of a large olive, sweet to the taste and with very little acidity.

Imperial (Metric)	American
½ pint (300ml) Rosé de Provence	1⅓ cups Rosé de Provence wine
3 oz (75g) sugar	½ cup sugar
2 teaspoons agar powder	2 teaspoons agar powder
Juice of 1 lemon	Juice of 1 lemon
12 mirabelles, halved and stoned	12 mirabelles, halved and pitted
12 sour cherries, stoned	12 sour cherries, pitted
3 fl oz (90ml) double cream	⅓ cup heavy cream

1 Bring the wine gently to the boil with the sugar. Add the agar powder and boil for 2 minutes. Stir in the lemon juice.

2 Add the mirabelles and let them soak in the hot liquid. As it cools, add the cherries. Before the mixture sets, remove the fruit with a slotted spoon.

3 Set half the jelly in four tall glasses. Spoon the fruit over this.

4 Reheat the remaining jelly if necessary, then pour over the fruit, so that is is suspended in jelly, halfway up the glasses.

5 Whip the cream and pipe rosettes on the top of each glass, then serve.

Mousseline de Banane aux Grenadilles

BANANA MOUSSE WITH PASSION FRUIT

Serves 6

Bananas and rum are one of the great combinations, but it is a heady mixture that needs to be offset with an aromatic sharpness, such as that of the passion fruit. These light mousses are second cousin to the jelly. They are set, but they are a creamy opaque; smooth, but with the contrast of an occasional bite from chopped nuts and crystallized fruit. The passion fruit is a sauce in itself, since it simply needs to be halved and scooped to produce a silky, coating liquid dotted with tiny edible seeds. What a perfect combination!

Imperial (Metric)	American
4 ripe bananas, peeled	4 ripe bananas, peeled
Juice and grated rind of ½ lemon	Juice and grated rind of ½ lemon
2 tablespoons clear honey	2 tablespoons clear honey
2 tablespoons white rum	2 tablespoons white rum
½ pint (300ml) natural yogurt	1⅓ cups plain yogurt
3 tablespoons water	3 tablespoons water
1 tablespoon agar-agar powder	1 tablespoon agar-agar powder
2 eggs, separated	2 eggs, separated
2 tablespoons chopped almonds	2 tablespoons chopped almonds
1 tablespoon chopped angelica	1 tablespoon chopped angelica
6 passion fruits	6 passion fruits

1 Chop the bananas and place in a blender goblet with the lemon juice and rind, honey and rum. Blend until smooth.

2 Turn out into a bowl and stir in the yogurt.

3 Heat the water to boiling, stir in the agar powder and boil for 3 minutes. Beat into the mixture. Then beat in the egg yolks.

4 Whisk the egg whites. As the mixture is on the point of setting, fold in the egg whites – lightly but thoroughly.

5 Spoon the mixture into 6 individual, greased ramekins, or a single greased loaf tin. Chill until set – about 4 hours.

6 Halve the passion fruit and scoop out onto 6 plates. Unmould a mousse onto each and serve at once.

Mousse de Reine-Claudes au Chocolat

GREENGAGE MOUSSE IN CHOCOLATE CUPS

Makes 16–20

Sir William Gage of Suffolk brought the greengage from the monastery of Chartreuse to my adopted land of England, and gave it his name. Thus, it is only appropriate to use in a greengage dish that very special liqueur, made by the Carthusian monks of Chartreuse. Made with 130 herbs, its flavour is unique.

Imperial (Metric)	American
14 oz (400g) plain chocolate	14 ounces baker's chocolate
2 teaspoons agar-agar powder	2 teaspoons agar-agar powder
2 tablespoons water	2 tablespoons water
½ pint (300ml) puréed stewed greengages	1⅓ cups puréed stewed greengages
½ pint (300ml) natural yogurt	1⅓ cups plain yogurt
2 tablespoons yellow Chartreuse	2 tablespoons yellow Chartreuse

1 Melt the chocolate, and use to coat 16–20 paper cake cases (use 3 cases together for each, to get a sufficient thickness and strength). Allow to cool, then coat again. Chill.
2 Dissolve the agar in the water. Bring to a boil, and boil for 3 minutes before beating into the greengage purée. Then fold in the yogurt and liqueur.
3 Just as the mixture starts to set, spoon into the chocolate cups. Allow to set before serving.

Volupté Nuptiale aux Framboises

RASPBERRY CREAM WITH EAU DE VIE

Serves 4

The potent liqueurs of Alsace, called *eau de vie* are flavoured with various fruits, raspberry being one of my favourites. This 'water of life' is well suited to the raspberry, since it is a fruit well known for its healing qualities. Raspberry leaf tea, with its astringent qualities, is good for sore throats, as a wash for wounds, and for settling stomach complaints. A spoonful of raspberry vinegar in a glass of warm water is a refreshing and stimulating drink, guaranteed to awaken even the sleepiest head in the morning!

Imperial (Metric)	American
5 oz (150g) silken tofu	Scant cup silken tofu
1 tablespoon clear honey	1 tablespoon clear honey
1½ lb (750g) fresh raspberries	1½ pounds fresh raspberries
2 tablespoons framboise eau de vie	2 tablespoons framboise eau de vie
3 egg whites	3 egg whites
1 tablespoon caster sugar	1 tablespoon superfine sugar
Slices of pawpaw and orange, to decorate	Slices of papaya and orange, to decorate
Extra raspberries, to garnish	Extra raspberries, to garnish

1 Blend the tofu with the honey until smooth. Turn into a bowl.

2 Purée the raspberries and liqueur, then pass through a strainer to remove the seeds. Stir the purée into the tofu mixture.

3 Whip the egg whites with the sugar until stiff, then fold carefully into the fruit and tofu mixture.

4 Spoon into four tall cocktail-type glasses and decorate with the fruit. Serve at once.

Crème de Cerises au Yaourt Montmorency

GELLED CHERRY-YOGURT CREAM

Serves 6

In Spring, the cherry-growing regions of France are white with blossom, and the harvest of that beauty comes in July, when the fruits are ripe – from the large white varieties, such as Coeur de Pigeon, Jaboulay, Marmottes de l'Yonne and Napoléon; through the soft, sweet-fleshed Précoces de la Manche and Actives de Bales; to the acid Griottes and Morellos, used for cooking and pickling. Of the latter, the finest are grown, and named for, Montmorency near Paris.

The cherries for this recipe must be soaked in the Kirsch syrup for a week before use.

Imperial (Metric)	American
2 lb (1 kilo) Montmorency cherries	2 pounds cooking cherries
12 oz (350g) clear honey	1 cup clear honey
½ pint (300ml) Kirsch	1⅓ cups Kirsch
1 stick cinnamon	1 stick cinnamon
6 fl oz (180ml) Greek yogurt	¾ cup Greek yogurt
1 teaspoon agar-agar powder	1 teaspoon agar-agar powder
¼ pint (150ml) double cream	⅔ cup heavy cream

1 Pit the cherries, then place in a jar with the honey, Kirsch and cinnamon. Stir well to mix, cover tightly and set aside for at least a week.

2 With a slotted spoon, remove 4 oz (100g/⅔ cup) cherries. Place in a blender with the yogurt and blend until smooth. Transfer to a bowl.

3 Pour 3 fl oz (90ml/⅓ cup) Kirsch syrup into a pan, sprinkle on the agar powder, bring to a boil and simmer for 3 minutes. Then stir into the cherry mixture and set aside to cool, stirring occasionally until nearly set.

4 Then fill six ramekins with the mixture and refrigerate until set.

5 For the sauce, blend 4 oz (100g/⅔ cup) cherries with 2 fl oz (60ml/¼ cup) Kirsch syrup.

6 Spoon a little sauce onto each of six plates, then turn out a cherry cream onto each. Decorate with extra cherries. The remaining cherries in Kirsch can be saved for another time – or nibbled whenever you choose!

Tôt Fait de Pêches en Merveille

PEACH CHEESECAKE WITH COINTREAU

Serves 4

This dish was a favourite amongst my schoolfriends, when it was prepared by the Austrian pastry cook at my father's restaurant, the Buffet de la Halle in Boulogne. Parents, teachers and boys would gather once a week, on Sunday for a meal. We even loaned one of our best chefs to the College, and so popular was the improved cuisine that the grateful rector asked my father if he could stay for good! He did so, and remained there until his death twenty years later. Perhaps one of the reasons that the French appreciate good food so much is that they are exposed to it from a very early age.

Imperial (Metric)	*American*
For the base	**For the base**
6 oz (175g) ginger biscuits	*1 cup ginger biscuits*
4 oz (100g) butter	*½ cup butter*
For the topping	**For the topping**
2 eggs	*2 eggs*
2 tablespoons dark honey	*2 tablespoons dark honey*
1 ripe peach	*1 ripe peach*
Juice of 2 lemons	*Juice of 2 lemons*
2 tablespoons Cointreau	*2 tablespoons Cointreau*
1 teaspoon agar-agar powder	*1 teaspoon agar-agar powder*
1 lb (450g) Quark or Ricotta	*1 pound Quark or Ricotta*
1 oz (25g) caster sugar	*2 tablespoons superfine sugar*

1 Place the biscuits in a paper bag and roll over it several times with a rolling pin to crush evenly.

2 Melt the butter in a pan and stir in the crumbs. Spoon into the base of a greased, loose-bottomed cake tin and press down firmly. Refrigerate until needed.

3 Separate the eggs and beat the yolks and honey in a double boiler until light and creamy. Remove from the heat.

4 Skin, halve and stone the peach. Blend with the lemon juice and Cointreau, then place the purée in a pan. Stir in the agar and bring to the boil. Simmer for 10 minutes, then allow to cool.

5 In a bowl, beat together the egg yolk mixture and the cheese, then stir in the thickening peach purée.

6 Whisk the egg whites with the sugar until stiff. Fold, little by little, into the peach mixture, then spoon over the ginger biscuit base.

7 Refrigerate the cheesecake until firm, then turn out carefully and serve. If wished, the top can be glazed with melted apricot jam and sprinkled with toasted flaked almonds or fresh redcurrants.

Crème Brulée au Cassis

BLACKCURRANT BRULÉE

Serves 4

Despite its French name, this dish stems from an invention of Trinity College, Cambridge, of some three hundred years ago. Nowadays, in looking to reduce the richness of our desserts, it is often, as here, married with sharp fruits, and the richness is cut yet further by substituting yogurt for part or all of the original cream.

Choose a fruit yogurt of very high quality for this dish, not one of those synthetic, highly-coloured concoctions so often found on the supermarket shelves. If you cannot find anything of superior quality, substitute plain Greek yogurt.

Imperial (Metric)	*American*
10 oz (300g) fresh or frozen blackcurrants	*1⅔ cups fresh or frozen blackcurrants*
8 tablespoons water	*8 tablespoons water*
A little sugar, to taste	*A little sugar, to taste*
2 level teaspoons cornflour	*2 level teaspoons cornstarch*
A little sugar, to taste	*A little sugar, to taste*
½ pint (300ml) blackcurrant yogurt	*1⅓ cups blackcurrant yogurt*
4 heaped teaspoons raw cane sugar	*4 heaped teaspoons raw cane sugar*
1 oz (25g) flaked almonds	*¼ cup slivered almonds*

1 Place the washed berries in a pan with the water. Cover and cook gently until soft. Spoon out a little of the liquid and beat with the cornflour to make a smooth paste, then add this back into the pan.

2 Bring the berries to the boil and simmer for 1 or 2 minutes to thicken. Taste and sweeten accordingly. Set aside to cool.

3 Spoon the mixture into 4 ramekins, then spread yogurt over each one, to cover the berries completely.

4 Sprinkle sugar and almonds over each dish. Place under a very hot grill (broiler) to caramelize the sugar and toast the nuts.

5 Chill until the sugar topping has set, then serve.

CHAPTER SIX

Les Desserts Chauds de la Campagne et de la Forêt

Hot Desserts of the Fields and the Forests

The Loire region is understandably known as the Garden of France. Its rolling fields and orchards give us a wealth of the very best fruits – pears, apples, quinces, plums, apricots and peaches are bountiful in the orchards of the Touraine, Anjou and Orléans; its vines produce not only a range of wines from crisp Muscadet at its seaward end to heady Saumur and smoky Pouilly Fumé inland, but they also give us fine grapes for use as food as well; and its woodlands shelter berries of all sorts – wild foods that have been tamed and incorporated into our cuisine.

Many of our finest desserts hail, understandably, from this region. Clafoutis, Gâteau de Pithiviers, Tarte Tatin, macaroons and praline . . . the list of sweetness is endless. And Blois is a mecca for the chocolate lover, while further downstream the fairytale château of Chenonceaux is owned by the Menier family, whose chocolate is synonymous with excellence for those who appreciate this favourite food.

This favoured region, so steeped in history

and so glorious to look at with its natural beauty and the best that architects have achieved as a gilding of the lily, is thus a joy for the senses in all ways. Few pleasures can exceed that of sitting, in the heat of a late afternoon in high Summer, in the shade of a café on the bank of one of the great Loire's little tributaries, head reeling from the sights of the châteaux or perhaps Leonardo's last home at Amboise. The Patron offers no menu. Rather, he brings, unasked but so welcome, a chilled glass of his own reserve wine, and a generous stack of little yeasted cakes, glistening with berries, topped with unctuous cream and frosted with a dusting of sugar. He pulls up a chair, pours his own glassful of wine, and talks to you about food, about history, and the two are interwoven as they always have been. Later, a cup of good, fresh coffee sends you refreshed into the early evening, full of the smells of river water on ancient stone, the drift of incense and candle wax from a centuries-old church, and the first aromas of the evening's dinners,

91

cooking in a hundred different eating places. The spell of the region washes over you like a great heartbeat – this, then is the ripe fruit of France, in all its glory.

Gaufres des Ardennes

BUTTERMILK ORANGE WAFFLES

Makes 12

In most towns in Northern France, you will find an annual fair with music, dancing, parades and feasting. Street vendors sell many delicious titbits to help keep up your energy for the festivities, and especially popular are these little waffles, served with ripe berries, or spread with jam or honey, a dash of liqueur and a dusting of sugar.

Imperial (Metric)	*American*
½ oz (15g) fresh yeast	*1 heaping tablespoon fresh yeast*
2 tablespoons warm water	*2 tablespoons warm water*
3 eggs, beaten	*3 eggs, beaten*
1 oz (25g) caster sugar	*2 tablespoons caster sugar*
1 lb (450g) wholemeal flour	*4 cups whole wheat flour*
Pinch sea salt	*Pinch sea salt*
1 oz (25g) ground almonds	*¼ cup ground almonds*
¼ pint (150ml) buttermilk	*⅔ cup buttermilk*
4 oz (100g) butter, melted	*½ cup butter, melted*
6 drops orange blossom water	*6 drops orange blossom water*
6 drops vanilla essence	*6 drops vanilla essence*
Vegetable oil, for cooking	*Vegetable oil, for cooking*
1 lb (450g) fresh raspberries	*1 pound fresh raspberries*
Fruit liqueur	*Fruit liqueur*
Caster sugar, to dust	*Superfine sugar, to dust*

1 Crumble the yeast onto the water and blend together. Stir in the eggs and sugar, then sprinkle on a little flour. Leave to ferment for 15 minutes.

2 When the mixture has begun to bubble, beat in the rest of the flour, the salt, buttermilk, melted butter, orange and vanilla flavourings. Cover with a cloth and leave to prove for 2 hours. Then beat well.

3 Heat a waffle iron and brush both sides with oil. Spoon on some of the batter and cook for 3 to 4 minutes, until golden on both sides. Unmould onto kitchen paper towels and keep warm.

4 To serve, place clean berries onto each waffle, splash on a dash of fruit-based liqueur and dust with caster sugar. If wished, the waffles could be placed briefly under a hot grill (broiler) to glaze the sugar. Serve with thick cream.

Volupté Gauloise

BLUEBERRY YEAST CAKES

Serves 4

France is a centre of gastronomy that attracts the very best chefs of all nations to its shores. And, as much as they come to learn from us, we can, if we are wise, learn also from them. Just such a case was that of our Austrian pastry cook, who worked for my father for five years, learning both the French language and French cuisine during his time with us. We, too, learned much from him – his wonderful desserts became a part of our best menus, and this one, in particular, has stayed in my own repertoire for a full forty-five years or more.

Imperial (Metric)	American
8 oz (225g) wholemeal flour	2 cups whole wheat flour
½ oz (12g) fresh yeast	1 heaping tablespoon fresh yeast
¼ pint (150ml) skimmed milk	⅔ cup skimmed milk
2 eggs, beaten	2 eggs, beaten
Pinch sea salt	Pinch sea salt
½ oz (12g) melted butter	2 teaspoons melted butter
1 teaspoon clear honey	1 teaspoon clear honey
Extra butter, for frying	Extra butter, for frying

For the filling:	**For the filling:**
8 oz (225g) blueberries	1⅓ cups blueberries
2 fl oz (60ml) red wine	¼ cup red wine
2 oz (50g) raw cane sugar	⅓ cup raw cane sugar
1 teaspoon arrowroot	1 teaspoon arrowroot
Pinch cinnamon	Pinch cinnamon
4 oz (100g) cream cheese	½ cup cream cheese
1 egg yolk	1 egg yolk
Grated rind and juice of 1 orange	Grated rind and juice of 1 orange
1 oz (25g) caster sugar	2 tablespoons superfine sugar
Chopped walnuts, to decorate	Chopped walnuts, to decorate

1 Place the flour in a bowl and make a well in the centre.
2 Mix the yeast with the warmed milk. Pour into the well, dust with flour and leave to ferment for 15 minutes, then blend in the eggs, salt, butter and honey. Beat well to a smooth dough, then leave in a warm place for 25 minutes. Beat again.

3 Meanwhile, poach the cleaned berries with the wine and sugar for 3 minutes. Spoon off a little of the juice, leave to cool for a few minutes, then mix with the arrowroot. Add this mixture back to the pan.

4 Bring this mixture back to the boil to thicken. Flavour with cinnamon and set aside to cool.

5 Beat together the cheese, egg, orange juice and rind.

6 Heat a little butter in a pan and make small pancakes with the batter, using about 2 tablespoonsful of batter per cake and cooking about 4 or 5 at a time. Cook on each side until golden and puffed up, then drain on kitchen paper towels.

7 Top half the pancakes with a spoonful of blueberry mixture, then cover with the remaining pancakes. Top these with the cheese mixture, dust with sugar, sprinkle with nuts and serve.

Note
Pitted black cherries could be used in place of the blueberries.

Illustrated opposite page 97.

Beignets d'Abricots aux Dames de Bretagne
APRICOT BUN FRITTERS

Serves 8

A dish for occasional use only, because these little fritters are deep-fried like doughnuts, but one which it would be a great shame to exclude, since it is quite superb! A little indulgence once in a while is good for the soul, and a generally healthy diet can afford the occasional lapse without doing you any harm, I'm sure.

Imperial (Metric)	*American*
1 recipe Roulade dough (page 116)	*1 recipe Roulade dough (page 116)*
5 ripe apricots	*5 ripe apricots*
Flour for dusting	*Flour for dusting*
2 ripe bananas, peeled and chopped	*2 ripe bananas, peeled and chopped*
3 tablespoons rum	*3 tablespoons rum*
2 fl oz (60ml) natural yogurt	*¼ cup plain yogurt*
Oil for frying	*Oil for frying*
Raw cane sugar to coat	*Raw cane sugar to coat*

1 Make up the dough as described on page 116.

2 Skin, halve and pit the apricots.

3 Dust a board with flour and roll out the dough to a thickness of 1 inch (2.5cm). Cut 16 circles, 3 inches (7.5cm) in diameter.

4 Place half an apricot on 8 of the dough circles. Wet the edges and lay another dough circle on top. Seal the edges tightly, shape into neat rounds and leave to prove for 20 minutes.

5 Make a sauce by placing the extra apricot in a blender with the bananas, rum and yogurt. Blend until smooth.

6 Heat sufficient polyunsaturated oil in a deep pan for deep frying. Fry the fritters, a few at a time, for 4 minutes. Drain onto kitchen paper towels, then toss in sugar and keep warm.

7 When all the fritters are cooked, spoon a little sauce onto each serving plate and place a fritter on each. Serve at once.

Opposite Nectarine and Chablis Ice (page 79).

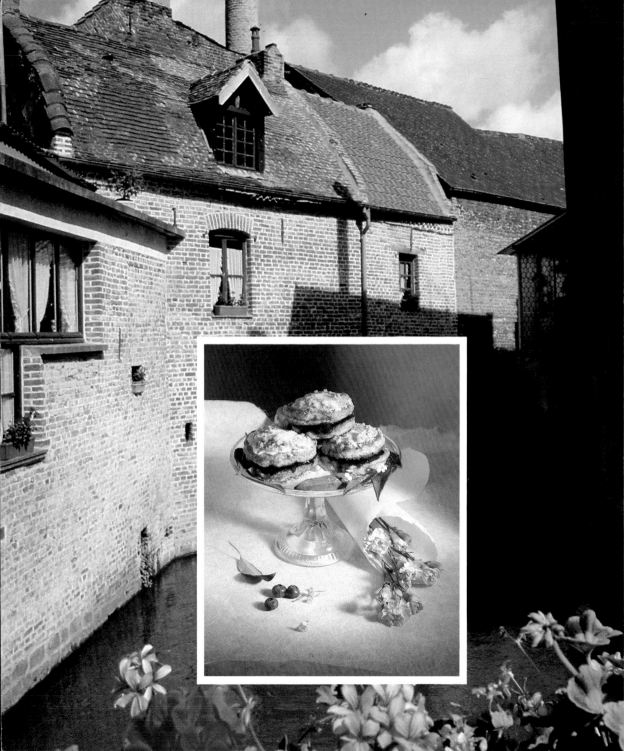

Nonettes de Fraises au Petit Lait

STRAWBERRY CHEESE DUMPLINGS

Makes 16

Here is another recipe in which a fruit secret hides at the centre of a simple dough, but this time the spiced curd cheese and breadcrumb dough is poached, and tucked inside each is a ripe strawberry, to delight your guests when the *nonette* is cut open.

Imperial (Metric)	American
8 oz (225g) fresh wholemeal breadcrumbs	4 cups fresh whole wheat breadcrumbs
4 oz (100g) curd cheese	½ cup curd cheese
1 oz (25g) caster sugar	2 tablespoons superfine sugar
Pinch sea salt	Pinch sea salt
2 oz (50g) butter, melted	¼ cup butter, melted
3 tablespoons natural yogurt	3 tablespoons natural yogurt
2 eggs, beaten	2 eggs, beaten
2 oz (50g) wholemeal flour	½ cup whole wheat flour
¼ teaspoon mixed spice	¼ teaspoon mixed spice
16 small, ripe strawberries	16 small, ripe strawberries

1 Beat the breadcrumbs with the cheese, then gradually beat in all the remaining ingredients except the strawberries, to form a firm, smooth dough. Leave the dough to rest for 30 minutes.
2 Wash, dry and hull the berries – choose only small, perfect berries for this dish.
3 Break the dough into 16 equal pieces, about the size of small eggs. Make a hole in the centre of each with your thumb, place a strawberry in each and mould the dough around it to seal completely.
4 Bring a pan of water to the boil, lower to a simmer and poach the dumplings for about 10 minutes – they will float to the surface as they cook. Remove with a slotted spoon, drain well, and place on plates coated with Strawberry and Orange Coulis (page 138). Serve at once.

Opposite Blueberry Yeast Cakes (page 94).

Les Crêpettes aux Mirabelles

YEASTED PANCAKES WITH MIRABELLES

Serves 4

This pancake recipe uses a yeast base, which produces a result similar to crumpets or English muffins. They are sandwiched with a fruit mixture – mirabelles (tiny golden plums), this time, flavoured with Port – and a dollop of sweetened fresh cheese. For an attractive presentation, push them down on one side to give a seashell effect.

Imperial (Metric)	American
1 oz (25g) fresh yeast	2½ tablespoons fresh yeast
2 fl oz (60ml) warm milk	¼ cup warm milk
1 lb (450g) wholemeal flour	4 cups whole wheat flour
¼ teaspoon sea salt	¼ teaspoon sea salt
¼ teaspoon sugar	¼ teaspoon sugar
½ teaspoon cinnamon	½ teaspoon cinnamon
2 eggs, beaten	2 eggs, beaten
½ pint (300ml) buttermilk	1⅓ cups buttermilk

For the filling	For the filling
8 oz (225g) mirabelles	8 oz (225g) mirabelles
2 fl oz (60ml) Port	2 fl oz (60ml) Port
2 oz (50g) honey	2 oz (50g) honey
½ teaspoon cornflour	½ teaspoon cornflour
6 oz (150g) curd cheese	6 oz (150g) curd cheese
2 fl oz (60ml) double cream, whipped	2 fl oz (600ml) double cream, whipped
2 egg whites, whisked	2 egg whites, whisked

1 Crumble the yeast into the warm milk, and blend until smooth.
2 In a bowl, mix together the flour, salt, sugar and cinnamon. Make a well in the centre and pour in the yeast mixture. Leave to ferment, covered in a little flour, for 15 minutes, then stir in the eggs and buttermilk. Mix to a smooth batter.
3 Halve and pit the mirabelles, and poach in the Port and honey until soft. Strain off a little of the juice and mix with the cornflour. Add back to the plums and heat to thicken. Set aside.
4 Beat together the cheese, whipped cream and whisked egg whites.

5 In a large, oiled pan, fry little pancakes, six at a time, until golden and risen on each side. Remove to kitchen paper towels to drain off any fat.

6 Place one spoonful of fruit mixture onto half the pancakes. Spoon a little of the cheese mixture over this. Place one of the remaining pancakes over each, pressing down firmly on one side. If wished, a little sugar can be sifted over each before serving.

Banane et Ananas au Muesli

BANANA AND PINEAPPLE CRUMBLE

Serves 4

This luscious and healthy dish has many uses. As a dessert, of course, it is a rich and flavourful treat with which to finish the meal. But it can be a breakfast dish, too, for it combines those very ingredients the experts tell us will provide vitality for the day ahead – and it beats a cup of coffee and a bowl of cardboard-flavoured cereal hands down!

Imperial (metric)	American
4 bananas, peeled and cut in chunks	4 bananas, peeled and cut in chunks
4 slices fresh pineapple, cubed	4 slices fresh pineapple, cubed
Coarsely grated rind of 1 orange	Coarsely grated rind of 1 orange
2 tablespoons soft raw cane sugar	2 tablespoons soft raw cane sugar
5 oz (125g) wholemeal breadcrumbs	2 cups whole wheat breadcrumbs
3 oz (75g) butter	⅓ cup butter
2 tablespoons Demerara sugar	2 tablespoons Demerara sugar
2 tablespoons Muesli	2 tablespoons Muesli
Extra raw cane sugar, to glaze	Extra raw cane sugar, to glaze

1 Mix the chunks of banana and pineapple together with the orange rind and sugar. Place in a lightly greased baking dish.
2 Rub in the breadcrumbs and butter, then stir in the sugar and muesli. Sprinkle over the fruit and press down to cover the fruit evenly.
3 In an oven preheated to 375°F/190°C (Gas Mark 5), bake the pudding for 25–30 minutes. Remove and dust liberally with extra sugar.
4 Place under a hot grill (broiler) until the sugar is caramelized. Serve hot with thick Greek yogurt.

Les Poires au Chocolat Saint-Louis

PEAR AND CHOCOLATE CREAMS

Serves 6

Pears form the heart of many classic French desserts – poached in red wine as *Poires Belle-Angevine*, *Vigneronne* or *Richelieu*, in Port for *Poires Alma* and, perhaps most famous of all (and most popular, especially with children), served with ice-cream and hot chocolate sauce as *Poires Belle-Hélène*. This dish has echoes of a number of dishes, and the best qualities of each, with brioche as its base and chocolate-rum custard covering the pears, which poach in their own juices as the custard is baked.

Imperial (Metric)	American
2 small brioches	2 small brioches
2 ripe pears*	2 ripe pears*
1 pint (600ml) creamy milk	2½ cups creamy milk
4 oz (100g) plain chocolate	4 ounces plain chocolate
3 eggs, beaten	3 eggs, beaten
2 tablespoons rum	2 tablespoons rum

1 Cut the brioches into rounds to fit neatly into the bases of 6 greased ramekins.
2 Peel and core the pears, and cut into dice. Distribute between the 6 moulds.
3 Heat the milk and melt the chocolate in it. Allow to cool before beating in the eggs and rum – a little sugar may be added, to taste, if wished.
4 Pour the chocolate milk into the moulds, then place these in a baking tray and pour hot water into the tray to come half way up the sides of the ramekins.
5 Bake in the centre of a preheated oven at 400°F/200°C (Gas Mark 6) for 25 minutes. Serve hot, in their dishes, or cool to allow the little custards to be turned out.

* *Choose from Laurousse Agricole, Doyenne d'Hiver, Doyenne du Comice and Beurre Bachelier.*

Gratin de Raisins Noirs de Frontignan

GLAZED GRAPE CUSTARD

Serves 6

Grapes were cultivated, and wine made from them, in Egypt 4,000 years before Christ. It was the Phoenician traders who introduced vines to Greece, Italy, Spain and France. Today, 20 million acres of land are devoted to vineyards. Although Muscat grapes are generally accepted to be the best for desserts (and the wine made from them is indeed a nectar at its best, ideally suited to be served at the end of the meal), I prefer to use Sauvignon grapes in this particular recipe, as they contrast so well with the froth of brandied, creamy custard that covers them.

Imperial (Metric)	American
8 oz (225g) black seedless grapes	8 ounces black seedless grapes
4 egg yolks	4 egg yolks
1 egg white	1 egg white
4 oz (100g) caster sugar	⅔ cup superfine sugar
⅓ pint (200ml) double cream	¾ cup heavy cream
2 tablespoons cognac	2 tablespoons cognac
1 oz (25g) flaked almonds	¼ cup slivered almonds
Icing sugar, to glaze	Confectioner's sugar, to glaze

1 Skin and seed the grapes. Divide them between six lightly greased individual gratin dishes.
2 Place the egg yolks and white in a bowl and whisk in the sugar until thick and light.
3 Place the bowl over a pan of simmering water. Whisk in the cream and cognac and continue to whisk until the mixure is a thick, creamy sauce, greatly increased in volume. Pour the custard over the grapes.
4 Sprinkle each dish with almonds, then dust with sugar. Place under a hot grill (broiler) to glaze the tops. Serve at once.

Fondue au Chocolat

CHOCOLATE CREAM FONDUE WITH FRESH FRUITS

Serves 4

The noble Alpine dish of fondue is traditionally a savoury one – a lush, gently bubbling pot of cheese and wine into which cubes of stale bread are swirled on forks, before being consumed to keep the chill away on long Winter's nights; or a pan of sizzling oil for the quick frying of cubed meat, fish and vegetables; or even, in its 'Chinese' style, a pan of boiling stock into which similar ingredients are plunged to cook. But here is the dream of every chocolate-lover (and who is not?), a simple bowl of simmering, chocolate and liqueur cream, into which cubes of fresh fruit are dunked before they enchant the palate with their wonderful combination of fresh, sweet-sharp fruitiness and luxurious creaminess.

Imperial (Metric)	American
2 lb (1 kilo) ripe fruits of choice*, cleaned and cubed	2 pounds ripe fruit of choice*, cleaned and cubed
4 tablespoons Kirsch	4 tablespoons Kirsch
8 oz (225g) bitter chocolate	8 ounces bitter chocolate
2 tablespoons water	2 tablespoons water
2 tablespoons single cream	2 tablespoons single cream

1 Place the fruit in a bowl and marinate with half the Kirsch.

2 Melt the chocolate with the water in a small fondue pot (be careful to use a different one for a sweet fondue to that which you use for a savoury one – unless you like garlic-flavoured chocolate!). Stir in the cream and the rest of the Kirsch.

3 Drain off the liquid from the fruit (you may wish to add it to the pot later, to thin the chocolate down a little) and serve in a chilled bowl for your guests to spear onto forks and swirl in chocolate.

* Chocolate is an alkaline substance and acid fruits do not always 'marry' well with it. The best fruits to use are pears, bananas, and lychees. Some acid fruits can be used if they have been soaked in liqueur, such as brandied cherries.

Pain Perdu aux Fraises

FRENCH TOAST WITH STRAWBERRIES

Serves 4

This last dish introduces us to the next chapter, for it uses a fruit bread the recipe for which is yet to come. The French nature is one of frugality, and that has been responsible for many of the best dishes in our cuisine. The richness of the stock lies in the good ingredients that go into the pan – ingredients that others throw away. And this recipe, along with others you will encounter in the pages still to come, uses stale bread and transforms it into a real treat. So much a classic is this simple dish, that it has become known to other nations as French toast – and we are delighted to acknowledge it as our brainchild.

Imperial (Metric)	*American*
4 slices fruit bread	*4 slices fruit bread*
2 eggs, beaten	*2 eggs, beaten*
1 teaspoon rum	*1 teaspoon rum*
3 oz (75 g) butter, for frying	*⅓ cup butter, for frying*
8 oz (225 g) strawberries	*8 ounces strawberries*
2 tablespoons strawberry eau de vie	*2 tablespoons strawberry eau de vie*
1 teaspoon clear honey	*1 teaspoon clear honey*

1 Soak the bread in a mixture of beaten egg and rum for 1 minute.
2 Heat the butter in a pan and fry the bread on both sides until sizzling and golden. Drain on kitchen paper towels and keep warm.
3 Mash the cleaned, hulled strawberries with the eau de vie and honey, spread a little on each slice and serve at once. *Pain Perdu* becomes *Pain du Paradis* in an instant!

CHAPTER SEVEN

Les Entremets Légers à la Boulangère

Melt-in-the-Mouth Baked Fruit Desserts

In this chapter, you will find a variety of baked goods – pastries, cakes, batters, breads and bread-based desserts. Baking is a fundamental part of French cooking, from the baguettes, croissants and brioches that form a staple part of life, to those many dishes that carry the appellation *boulangère*, meaning that, in past times, they had been brought to the local baker's oven to cook by families who had no hot oven of their own. The French have always found great creative opportunities in the baking process, and here you will see just a fragment of such culinary imagination.

Flour is, in this chapter, the key to this creativity. All but the last four recipes use it in its natural form. The final four use the baked product of the baker's skill in a different form, and are testimony to the frugality of the French nature – why not make the most of good food, even when it has seemingly passed its best, by pairing it with fresh fruits, dairy produce and the like, and transforming it through the magic baking

process into a completely new meal?

For the rest, flour is the basis for breads, bakes, pastry and batter. Wholemeal or unbleached white, leavened with baking powder or yeast, or simply enriched with eggs, butter or milk, this amazingly versatile ingredient is in a class of its own. Every texture, every flavour is different, from crisp to doughy, from light to substantial, from rich to subtle – flour is the chameleon of the store cupboard.

One of the great treats of baking with flour is that there is no end to the varieties of ingredients that can be added to the basic ingredient. Here, for pastry, you will see that we have added a modicum of ground nuts or spices to lift a basic crust from the level of a container to that of a taste experience in itself. For bread or cake, the flour of choice can be augmented with fresh or dried fruits to give sweetness, texture and variety to a simple foodstuff. For any baked pudding, the produce of the granary is combined with the harvest of the orchard, dairy and woodland in

a cornucopia of excellence. Who needs arti-
ficial colours, flavours and the like, when this is so readily available to us? Not me – and not you either, I feel sure!

Les Napoléons d'Or

BAKED LEMONY YEAST CAKES

Serves 4

When Napoleon's son was born in Rome, the city of which he was later to be crowned king, the antecedents of these little cakes were baked in celebration. Their origin is thought to be Bohemian, and they are good served in the manner traditional to that region, with a brandied custard sauce and stewed apricots. Baked crisp and golden, to resemble Napoleon's francs, they are treasure indeed.

Imperial (Metric)	American
½ oz (15g) fresh yeast	½ ounce fresh yeast
2 fl oz (60ml) lukewarm water	¼ cup lukewarm water
2 oz (50g) sugar	⅓ cup sugar
10 oz (300g) wholemeal flour	2½ cups wholewheat flour
1 oz (25g) cornflour	¼ cup cornstarch
¼ teaspoon sea salt	¼ teaspoon sea salt
1 egg, beaten	1 egg, beaten
4 fl oz (120ml) buttermilk	½ cup buttermilk
2 oz (50g) melted butter	¼ cup melted butter
Grated rind 1 lemon	Grated rind 1 lemon
1 tablespoon vegetable oil	1 tablespoon vegetable oil
Extra butter, to glaze	Extra butter, to glaze

1 Dissolve the yeast in the water, add the sugar and leave to ferment for 15 minutes.
2 Sift together the flours and salt, and place in a low oven briefly to take off any chill. Make a well in the centre.
3 Pour the yeast mixture into the well and knead in, then knead in the buttermilk and melted butter. Knead thoroughly to form a smooth dough. Gather into a ball, cover and leave to prove in a warm place for 1 hour. Knock back and knead in the grated lemon rind. Leave to rest for 15 minutes.
4 Roll the dough out to a thickness of ½ inch (1cm). Cut 1 inch (2.5cm) rounds from this.
5 Brush the sides of each round with oil and lay, not too close together, on a greased baking tray (the oil will allow the rounds to be separated after baking). Brush the tops with melted butter. Leave to prove for 20 minutes.
6 Place in a preheated oven at 400°F/200°C (Gas Mark 6) for 15 minutes. Remove from the oven and lower the heat to 350°F/180°C (Gas Mark 4). Brush the tops again with melted butter and return to the oven to cook for a further 10 to 15 minutes, until crisp and golden. Serve with a custard sauce flavoured with apricot brandy, and apricots poached in a little honey and vermouth until tender.

Tourtes au Miel Montélimar

NUT AND SOUR CREAM TARTS

Serves 4

The town of Montélimar is renowned for its wonderful nougat, which suspends all sorts of nuts and fruits in a rich confection of honey-sweet, creamy delight. This recipe uses a simple and successful wholemeal pastry base – the secret is not to overknead the dough, and it is easiest to make individual tarts, so that if your pastry is crumbly, you can push it into shape, avoiding the tribulations of rolling out altogether!

Imperial (Metric)	American
For the pastry	**For the filling**
6 oz (150g) wholemeal flour	1½ cups whole wheat flour
Pinch sea salt	Pinch sea salt
3 oz (75g) unsalted butter	⅓ cup butter
1 egg	1 egg
For the filling	**For the filling**
3 eggs, separated	3 eggs, separated
¼ pint (150ml) sour cream	⅓ cup sour cream
¼ pint (150ml) clear honey	⅓ cup clear honey
1 level teaspoon agar-agar powder	1 level teaspoon agar-agar powder
1 tablespoon water	1 tablespoon water
1 tablespoon rum	1 tablespoon rum
2 oz (50g) chopped pecan nuts	1 cup chopped pecan nuts
Pinch sea salt	Pinch sea salt
2 teaspoons caster sugar	2 teaspoons superfine sugar
1 ripe peach	1 ripe peach

1 Rub together the flour, salt and butter. Add the egg and mix to a smooth dough. Roll into a ball, cover with clingfilm (saran wrap) and chill for 20 minutes.

2 Divide the dough into four pieces, flatten to fit greased moulds about 4 inches (10cm) in diameter. Prick the bases with a fork and bake at 400°F/200°C (Gas Mark 6) for 20 minutes. Allow to cool.

3 Meanwhile, make the filling. Beat the egg yolks into the sour cream, then stir in the honey.

4 Sprinkle the agar onto the water and rum in a pan, then bring to a boil and boil for a few minutes. Beat this into the cream mixture and transfer to a double boiler. Heat over simmering water, stirring constantly, until the mixture forms a smooth, thick cream. Remove from the heat and beat in the nuts.

5 Whisk the egg whites with the salt and sugar until they form stiff peaks. Fold into the cooled cream. Spoon into the pastry cases.

6 Skin, halve and pit the peaches, then cut into thin slivers. Use to decorate the tops of the tarts, then set in the refrigerator to chill for 2 hours before serving.

Galette de Poires aux Noix

PEAR AND NUT TART

Serves 4

Dessert pears, such as William, Doyenne de Comice and Bon Chretien are best for modern tastes because, when ripe, they are sweet and juicy and so little extra sugar (if any) is needed during cooking. Bergamot Espéren, Duchesse d'Angoulême and Louise-bonne d'Avranches varieties are also suitable. Pears were introduced to the British Isles by the Romans, and in the past the drink Perry, the pear equivalent of cider, was very popular. Perhaps it is time for a revival of interest in this drink which, to my mind, is superior to its apple-based cousin. This dessert combines pears with a delicate and delicious pastry speckled with the greens and golds of ground pistachio nuts.

Imperial (Metric)	American
For the pastry	**For the pastry**
8 oz(225g) plain flour	2 cups plain flour
2 oz (50g) ground pistachio nuts	½ cup ground pistachio nuts
1 tablespoon icing sugar	1 tablespoon confectioner's sugar
Pinch sea salt	Pinch sea salt
5 oz (125g) butter	Heaping ½ cup butter
1 egg yolk	1 egg yolk
For the pastry cream	**For the pastry cream**
2 oz (50g) caster sugar	¼ cup superfine sugar
1 egg	1 egg
1 egg yolk	1 egg yolk
½ oz (15g) plain flour	1 tablespoon plain flour
¾ oz (20g) cornflour	Heaping tablespoon cornstarch
½ pint (300ml) milk	⅔ cup milk
Few drops vanilla essence or 1 tablespoon liqueur	Few drops vanilla essence or 1 tablespoon liqueur
For the topping	**For the topping**
3 ripe pears	3 ripe pears
Juice of 1 lemon	Juice of 1 lemon
4 tablespoons apricot jam	4 tablespoons apricot jam
2 tablespoons toasted flaked almonds	2 tablespoons toasted slivered almonds

1 Mix together the flour, nuts, salt and sugar in a bowl. Rub in the butter, then mix in the egg yolk to form a smooth pastry dough. Wrap in clingfilm (saran wrap) and chill for 1 hour.

2 Meanwhile, prepare the pastry cream. Beat together the sugar with the eggs, then beat in the flours, adding a little of the milk if needed to form a smooth paste.

3 Heat the remaining milk in a pan, then beat the hot milk into the paste before returning the entire mixture to the pan. Stir over a low heat until thickened and smooth. Set aside to cool.

4 Roll out the chilled dough and use to line a 9 inch (23cm) loose-bottomed flan tin. Line with baking paper and baking beans and bake blind at 190°F/375°C (Gas Mark 5) for 10 minutes. Remove the paper and beans and return to the oven to bake for a further 12–15 minutes. Allow to cool.

5 Beat the cooled pastry cream with the liqueur (Poire William is good, but you could use Kirsch as a substitute) and then spread this evenly over the base of the tart.

6 Peel, halve and core the pears, and toss in about half the lemon juice. Drain well and arrange attractively, radiating out from the centre of the tart.

7 Melt the jam with another spoonful or so of the lemon juice, then spread over the top of the tart. Sprinkle with nuts, then allow the jam to cool and set. Serve cool, but not chilled.

Tarte aux Mures d'Autonne

BLACKBERRY AND HAZEL TART

Serves 8

My family in Amiens produces an annual harvest of blackberry jam and – even better – blackberry liqueur. I recall, from my youth, the excitement of the expeditions into the early morning mists to gather both fat blackberries and fresh hazelnuts from the woodlands, and the satisfaction of returning to the kitchen with baskets full of the Autumn's goodness. This tart is typical of the delicious results of those forays into the French countryside, and it can be recreated in your own kitchen, wherever your home may be.

Imperial (Metric)
For the pastry
4 oz (100g) wholemeal flour
1 oz (25g) cornflour
2 oz (50g) Muscovado sugar
3 oz (75g) ground, toasted hazelnuts
Good pinch mixed spice
4 oz (100g) unsalted butter
1 egg

For the filling
4 oz (100g) bitter chocolate
12 oz (350g) cream cheese
6 oz (150g) cottage cheese
3 large eggs, separated
4 fl oz (120ml) cider
1 teaspoon agar-agar
3 oz (75g) raw cane sugar
Juice and grated rind of 1 orange
Pinch sea salt
1 lb (450g) blackberries

American
For the pastry
1 cup whole wheat flour
2 tablespoons cornstarch
⅓ cup Muscovado sugar
¾ cup ground, toasted hazelnuts
Good pinch mixed spice
½ cup unsalted butter
1 egg

For the filling
4 ounces bitter chocolate
1½ cups cream cheese
¾ cup farmer's cheese
3 large eggs, separated
½ cup cider
1 teaspoon agar-agar
½ cup raw cane sugar
Juice and grated rind of 1 orange
Pinch sea salt
1 pound blackberries

1 In a bowl, mix together the flours, sugar, nuts and spices. Rub in the butter, and then mix in the egg to form a smooth dough. Roll into a ball, wrap in clingfilm (saran wrap) and chill for 25 minutes.
2 Preheat the oven to 400°F/200°C (Gas Mark 6). Place the dough between two sheets of greaseproof (parchment) paper. Gently roll out into a round of 8 inches (20cm) diameter, remove, and then slip it

112

into a loose-bottomed flan tin and press it to fit. Bake for 15 minutes. Leave to cool before removing.

3 Melt the chocolate in a double boiler and brush the insides of the pastry case to cover completely.

4 Beat together the two cheeses, then push through a sieve to blend and smooth. Beat in the egg yolks.

5 In a pan, heat the cider and sprinkle on the agar. Boil for 10 minutes, then add the sugar and orange juice and rind. Add to the cheese mixture, mix well and set aside to cool.

6 Beat the egg whites and salt to form stiff peaks. Fold into the cheese mixture, then spoon into the pastry case and smooth out. Leave to set for at least 2 hours.

7 Wash and drain the blackberries. Arrange over the top of the tart to cover neatly. If wished, the berries could be glazed with a little melted jam before serving. When completely cold, remove the tart from the tin and serve.

Flamiche de Montdidier

PLUM SCONE CAKE WITH ALMOND CREAM

Serves 6

One of our most famous desserts is the almond cream gâteau from Pithiviers, a small town in the outskirts of the Loire valley. Then we have the famous Tarte Normande, its light sweet pastry covered with almond cream before being topped with thinly sliced apples and glazed with conserve. The dish we give here fills a scone-type pastry with almond cream and tops it with plums which are glazed with quince jelly. It comes from the little town of Montdidier in northern France – so typical of the small communities, dotted about all over the country, where people care about the traditions of good, local cooking. We owe our great heritage of French cuisine to places such as these.

Imperial (Metric)	American
For the pastry	**For the pastry**
1 lb (450g) self-raising wholemeal flour	*4 cups self-rising whole wheat flour*
3 oz (75g) raw cane sugar	*½ cup raw cane sugar*
3 oz (75g) butter	*Heaping ⅓ cup butter*
2 eggs, beaten	*2 eggs, beaten*
Cornflour, to dust	*Cornstarch, to dust*
Vegetable oil, to grease pan	*Vegetable oil, to grease pan*
For the filling	**For the filling**
2 oz (50g) butter	*¼ cup butter*
2 oz (50g) caster sugar	*⅓ cup superfine sugar*
2 oz (50g) ground almonds	*½ cup ground almonds*
1 oz (25g) crushed toasted hazels	*¼ cup crushed toasted hazels*
1 egg, beaten	*1 egg, beaten*
2 fl oz (60ml) brandy	*¼ cup brandy*
8 oz (50g) ripe plums	*8 ounces ripe plums*
1 teaspoon agar-agar	*1 teaspoon agar-agar*
5 tablespoons water	*5 tablespoons water*
2 oz (50g) quince jelly	*2 tablespoons quince jelly*
1 oz (25g) toasted flaked almonds	*¼ cup toasted slivered almonds*

1 In a bowl, mix together the flour and sugar, then rub in the butter. Stir in the beaten egg to form a smooth dough, and roll into a ball.

114

2 Halve the dough, and roll out one half on a board, dusted with flour, to a diameter of 7 inches (18cm) then use to line the base of a greased and floured loose-bottomed cake tin.

3 Roll the remaining dough into a strip 2 inches (5cm) wide. Use this to line the sides of the tin, pinching to seal to the base.

4 For the filling, cream the butter with the sugar, then beat in the nuts, and then the beaten egg and brandy, to form a smooth cream. spread this evenly over the base of the dough.

5 Skin, halve and pit the plums. Lay them attractively over the almond cream. Place in a preheated oven at 375°F/190°C (Gas Mark 5) and bake for about 1 hour, or until cooked through.

6 Meanwhile, sprinkle the agar onto the water and boil for 5 minutes, then add the jelly and melt together. Set aside to cool a little before pouring over the plums. Sprinkle with toasted almonds, then leave to cool completely before serving.

Roulade de Pruneaux d'Agen

PLUM AND APPLE ROLL WITH ARMAGNAC

Serves 8

Prunes are a much neglected dried fruit, all too often associated with invalid food, or dreaded school dinners. Yet, used imaginatively, the dried plum can add a richness of flavour to a dish that is rather special. In this spicy roulade, they are matched with the sharpness of apples, the bite of walnuts, and the warmth of spices, all rolled up in a satisfying bun dough – delicious!

Imperial (Metric)	*American*
For the dough	**For the dough**
⅔ oz (18g) fresh yeast	2 tablespoons fresh yeast
¼ pint (150ml) mixed milk and water	⅓ cup mixed milk and water
1 oz (25g) honey	2 tablespoons honey
8 oz (225g) wholemeal flour	2 cups whole wheat flour
Pinch sea salt	Pinch sea salt
1 oz (25g) cornflour	¼ cup cornstarch
2 oz (50g) butter	¼ cup butter
For the filling	**For the filling**
4 oz (100g) chopped soaked prunes	1 cup chopped soaked prunes
4 oz (100g) thinly sliced apples	1 cup thinly sliced apples
4 oz (100g) chopped walnuts	1 cup chopped walnuts
3 oz (75g) raw cane sugar	½ cup raw cane sugar
1 teaspoon mixed spice	1 teaspoon mixed spice
2 tablespoons Armagnac or Calvados	2 tablespoons Armagnac or Calvados
Beaten egg to glaze	*Beaten egg to glaze*

1 In a bowl, cream together the yeast, milk and water, and honey. Leave in a warm place to ferment for 10 minutes.

2 Preheat the oven to 400°F/200°C (Gas Mark 6). Place the flours and salt in a bowl, and place this in the oven for 4 minutes to warm.

3 Blend the yeast ferment into a well in the warmed flour and knead well to form an elastic dough. Gather into a ball, cover the bowl with a cloth, and leave to prove for 30 minutes.

4 Knock back the risen dough and knead in the butter.

5 Lightly flour a pastry board and roll out the dough to form an oblong ¼ inch (5 mm) thick. Lay the fruit over the dough, then sprinkle with nuts, sugar and liqueur. Roll the dough up from the longer side, pinching the edges to seal in the filling. Place on a greased baking tray, seamed side down. Cover with a dampened cloth and leave to prove for 30 minutes.

6 Glaze the roll with beaten egg and place in a preheated oven at 400°F/200°C (Gas Mark 6) on the middle shelf. Bake for 35 to 40 minutes, until golden.

7 Leave to cool before slicing into pretty rounds. Serve with soured cream.

Note
The prunes can be soaked in whatever liquid you choose, but tea is a good choice, as is fruit juice with a dash of liqueur.

Illustrated opposite page 128.

Bisette d'Auzais

BAKED RAISIN AND PEACH CRÊPE DESSERT

Serves 8

I spent many of my school holidays in a little village near Fontenay le Comte, where I was born during World War I. The relatives with whom I stayed had a farm, on which they made their own butter, cream and cheese. This dish, using butter with a tang of lactic acid, and soured cream, was one of the many delicious desserts with which Madame Coulais, my Godmother, used to treat the neighbourhood children at tea-time.

Imperial (Metric)	American
For the batter	**For the batter**
4 oz (100g) self-raising wholemeal flour	1 cup self-rising whole wheat flour
Pinch sea salt	Pinch sea salt
2 eggs, beaten	2 eggs, beaten
½ pint (300ml) buttermilk	1⅓ cups buttermilk
1 oz (25g) butter	2 tablespoons butter
For the filling	**For the filling**
	3 eggs, beaten
6 fl oz (180ml) sour cream	¾ cup sour cream
4 fl oz (120ml) clear honey	½ cup clear honey
4 oz (100g) seedless raisins	⅔ cup seedless raisins
1 teaspoon mixed spice	1 teaspoon mixed spice
Juice and grated rind 1 lemon	Juice and grated rind 1 lemon
1 tablespoon peach liqueur	1 tablespoon peach liqueur
8 peaches, skinned, halved and stoned	8 peaches, skinned, halved and pitted

1 First, prepare the batter. Place the flour in a bowl with the salt. In another bowl, beat together the eggs and buttermilk, then gradually blend this mixture into the flour to form a smooth mixture.
2 Melt a little of the butter in a pan, make 6 to 8 thin pancakes and lay them aside to cool.
3 Grease a loose-based 9 inch (23cm) cake tin. Line the base and sides with the pancakes, trimming them into ribbons if necessary so that the sides are neatly lined.
4 For the filling, beat together all the remaining ingredients except the peaches. Pour half the mixture into the pancake-lined tin.
5 Place in a preheated oven at 400°F/200°C (Gas Mark 6) for about 20 minutes, or until the filling has set (this will prevent the filling seeping through the lining). Then add the rest of the filling and bake for a further 15 minutes, or until set.

6 If the peaches are not perfectly ripe, grill or poach them briefly while the *bisette* is baking.

7 Cool and then chill the dessert before removing carefully from the tin, then arrange the peaches neatly on top and serve. If you prefer, the peaches could be arranged on top whilst the dessert is still in the tin, and slices cut from there.

Gâteau aux Pommes et Poires de la Somme

APPLE AND PEAR YOGURT CAKE

Serves 4

This dessert was made by my Grandmother Mathilde when I was a child. I have replaced the creamy milk she used with yogurt, to give a lighter batter and a more piquant taste, but half-and-half yogurt and cream is a good mixture, too.

Imperial (Metric)	American
1 large or 2 small eggs	1 large or 2 small eggs
2 fl oz (60ml) clear honey	2 good tablespoons clear honey
½ pint (300ml) natural yogurt	1⅓ cups plain yogurt
2 tablespoons milk	2 tablespoons milk
3 oz (75g) wholemeal flour	¾ cup whole wheat flour
½ oz (15g) baking powder	1 teaspoon baking powder
1 tablespoon Calvados	1 tablespoon Calvados
1 large apple	1 large apple
1 large pear	1 large pear
1 oz (25g) icing sugar	¼ cup confectioner's sugar
Good pinch cinnamon	Good pinch cinnamon

1 Beat together the egg, honey, yogurt and milk in a large bowl. Sift in the flour and baking powder and mix to a smooth batter. Finally, mix in the Calvados.
2 Thinly slice the apple and pear, and mix into the batter.
3 Grease a mould, 7 inches (18cm) in diameter and 2 inches (5cm) deep, and pour in the fruit batter.
4 Place in a preheated oven at 400°F/200°C (Gas Mark 6), on the top shelf, and bake for 35 minutes or until risen and golden-brown.
5 Allow to cool a little before dusting with a mixture of sugar and cinnamon. Serve cold.

Pain de Campagne aux Fruits Secs

DRIED FRUIT BREAD

Makes 1 large loaf

This fruit bread was served daily at the Buffet de la Halle at breakfast time with café au lait, and in the afternoon with good farm butter and raspberry purée. It is also a good base for pain perdu, and other such recipes.

Imperial (Metric)	*American*
20 oz (550g) wholemeal flour	*5 cups whole wheat flour*
1 teaspoon soya flour	*1 teaspoon soy flour*
1 teaspoon sea salt	*1 teaspoon sea salt*
13 fl oz (375ml) warm water	*1²/₃ cups warm water*
½ oz (15g) fresh yeast	*1 heaping tablespoon fresh yeast*
1 teaspoon dark treacle	*1 teaspoon dark treacle*
2 oz (50g) seedless raisins	*⅓ cup seedless raisins*
2 oz (50g) sultanas	*⅓ cup golden seedless raisins*
2 oz (50g) glacéed orange peel	*⅓ cup glacéed orange peel*
1 teaspoon melted butter	*1 teaspoon melted butter*
2 oz (50g) seeds of choice	*⅓ cup seeds of choice*

1 Warm the flour briefly in a low oven – it should be at 77°F when used. Make a well in the centre.

2 Warm the water to 76°F and mix in the yeast and treacle. Set aside in a warm place for a few minutes to allow fermentation to begin.

3 Pour the yeast solution into the well in the warmed flour, and knead to a smooth dough. Roll into a ball, cover and leave in a warm place to prove for 30 minutes.

4 Meanwhile, soak the dried fruits in a little warm water to swell, then drain and pat dry.

5 Knock back the dough and knead in the butter, fruit and seeds (you could use sunflower, poppy, sesame or pumpkin for this). Mix well. Roll the dough into a neat oblong and place in a well-greased loaf tin. Cover and set aside to prove again for about 30 to 45 minutes – the dough should have risen well above the level of the tin.

6 Place on the middle shelf of a preheated oven at 450°F/230°C (Gas Mark 8) and bake for 30 minutes – if the loaf is browning too fast, you could lower the heat to 400°F/200°C (Gas Mark 6) after 10 minutes or so.

7 When the bread is cooked (test by tapping the bottom of the turned-out loaf, which should sound hollow) turn it out onto a wire rack to cool. Serve in any one of a number of ways, as suggested, including the following three satisfying baked desserts.

Pain de Cerises de Compiègne

CHERRY BREAD PUDDING

Serves 6

In the first of the fruit bread desserts, the bread is reduced to rich, fruit-speckled crumbs before being amalgamated with fat, ripe cherries and suspended in an eggy custard and soaked in cherry brandy – so simple a way to use up stale bread, yet so special!

Imperial (Metric)	American
1¼ pints (750ml) milk	3 cups milk
3 oz (75g) raw cane sugar	½ cup raw cane sugar
2 oz (50g) fruit bread crumbs	1 cup fruit bread crumbs
5 eggs, separated	5 eggs, separated
6 oz (150g) butter	¾ cup butter
1½ lb (750g) stoned black cherries	1½ pounds pitted black cherries
Pinch sea salt	Pinch sea salt
2 teaspoons caster sugar	2 teaspoons caster sugar
1 oz (25g) chopped nuts	¼ cup chopped nuts
2 fl oz (60ml) cherry brandy	¼ cup cherry brandy

1 Bring the milk and sugar to a boil, then remove from the heat.
2 Place the breadcrumbs in a bowl and pour the milk over them. Mix well and set aside to cool a little.
3 Beat the egg yolks and butter into the crumb mixture to mix, then stir in the cherries.
4 Whisk the egg whites with the salt and sugar, then fold lightly into the custard mixture.
5 Grease a dish, 2 inches (5cm) deep and 8 inches (20cm) in diameter. Pour the mixture into the dish and sprinkle with nuts.
6 Bake at 400°F/200°C (Gas Mark 6) for 35 minutes, then set aside to cool. Sprinkle with cherry brandy, leave to absorb, then unmould and serve with cream.

Pouding Diplomatique à la Boulonnaise

SPICED BREAD 'CASTLES' WITH RASPBERRIES

Serves 8

In the next recipe, the bread is cubed and combined with a simple spiced buttermilk custard, baked in individual moulds and served with a simple garnish of raspberries poached in Curaçao. It is worth baking an extra loaf and leaving it to get stale, for recipes such as these.

Imperial (Metric)	American
3 eggs, beaten	3 eggs, beaten
2 oz (50g) raw cane sugar	⅓ cup raw cane sugar
1 pint (300ml) buttermilk	2½ cups buttermilk
4 oz (100g) fruit bread, cut into small cubes	2 cups small cubes of fruit bread
8 oz (225g) fresh raspberries	1½ cups fresh raspberries
1 oz (25g) clear honey	2 tablespoons clear honey
1 fl oz (30ml) Curaçao	2 tablespoons Curaçao
Juice of ½ lemon	Juice of ½ lemon

1 In a bowl, beat together the eggs, sugar and buttermilk, then stir in the cubed fruit bread. Divide the mixture between 8 greased dariole moulds.
2 Set the moulds in a baking tray and fill with hot water to come half way up the sides of the moulds. Place in a preheated oven at 375°F/190°C (Gas Mark 5) and bake for 35 minutes.
3 Meanwhile, poach the cleaned raspberries in the honey, liqueur and lemon juice until tender.
4 Leave the cooked puddings to cool before turning out onto plates, and serve garnished with the poached berries.

Pouding de Pain au Rhum

RUM BREAD AND YOGURT DESSERT

Serves 4

This last dessert using stale fruit bread sees it sliced, soaked with rum, and used to line a dish that is then filled with a cinnamon-yogurt custard. It is very good served with a compote of pears or plums, or a layer of these fresh fruit could be placed in the base of the dish before the custard is poured on.

Imperial (Metric)	*American*
6 oz (150g) fruit bread	*6-ounce piece fruit bread*
3 tablespoons rum	*3 tablespoons rum*
3 eggs, beaten	*3 eggs, beaten*
2 tablespoons clear honey	*2 tablespoons clear honey*
1 teaspoon ground cinnamon	*1 teaspoon ground cinnamon*
1 pint (300ml) natural yogurt	*2½ cups plain yogurt*

1 Slice the bread thinly, then soak the slices in rum and use to line a pie dish completely, in one layer.
2 Beat together the eggs, honey, cinnamon and yogurt to form a smooth cream.
3 Pour the cream into the pie dish. Place the dish in a baking tray and add hot water to come half way up the side of the dish. Place in a preheated oven at 350°F/180°C (Gas Mark 4) for 40 minutes, until the custard is set. Serve as suggested above.

Les Croissants Conil aux Bananes Épicées

SPICED BANANA CROISSANTS

Serves 6

My son Christopher's special recipe for croissants was given in our first book, *Cuisine Végétarienne Française*, and these would be ideal for this particular recipe. Failing that, it is a wonderful way of using up stale croissants of any type.

Imperial (Metric)	American
3 bananas	*3 bananas*
Juice and grated rind of ½ lemon	*Juice and grated rind of ½ lemon*
2 tablespoons grounds almonds	*2 tablespoons ground almonds*
¼ teaspoon mixed spice	*¼ teaspoon mixed spice*
¼ teaspoon ground ginger	*¼ teaspoon ground ginger*
2 tablespoons chopped pecan nuts	*2 tablespoons chopped pecan nuts*
6 stale croissants	*6 stale croissants*
1 egg, beaten	*1 egg, beaten*
2 tablespoons flaked almonds	*2 tablespoons slivered almonds*

1 Peel and mash the bananas with the lemon juice and rind, ground almonds, spices and nuts.

2 Carefully split the croissants along the curved side to make a pocket in each. Fill with the spiced banana mixture. Lay on a greased baking sheet.

3 Place in a preheated oven at 375°F/190°C (Gas Mark 5) for 8 minutes. Serve straight from the oven for breakfast, with thick Greek yogurt to garnish.

CHAPTER EIGHT

Les Coulis et les Compotes Délicieux

A Garland of Sauces

The fruit sauce is an asset to an incredible variety of dishes, both savoury and sweet. We have already seen, in previous chapters, how fruit can bring to life a simple savoury dish. That elusive combination of tastes that constitutes the term 'piquant' is highly prized by chefs and gourmets, and it is perhaps most successfully achieved by the use of fruits to accent a dish. You will find sauces within these pages that, by just a tiny swirl on a plate before the food is served, will transform a good meal into an excellent one. Vegetarians might wish to try one of the berried sauces with a substantial terrine-type pulse-based dish; a sauce of peaches or plums with an unmoulded custard; one of the sweet-sour purées with a tofu or filo pastry recipe. Non-vegetarians will find that they are equally good with their chosen equivalent dishes.

The sweet dishes of earlier chapters are also exceptionally suited to the addition of a sauce. A small portion of flan, a sizzling pancake or a light soufflé can all be paired with a contrasting sauce to make the presentation

and flavour that bit extra-special.

Traditionally, the term *coulis* applies to a sauce that is made simply by the reduction or puréeing of the ingredients themselves, without the need for additional thickening ingredients. However, many fruit sauces intended for serving cold will benefit from a little help in stabilizing their ingredients. To this end, the sauces in this book can be prepared with or without the addition of a small quantity of cornflour (cornstarch) and water, in the proportion of 1 teaspoon of starch to 4 tablespoons of water. As much or as little of this slurry may be added to the sauce during cooking as is wished. If you prefer your sauce without this addition, then so be it – this ingredient may be viewed as optional in all the recipes where it is mentioned.

The final four recipes in this chapter are slightly different from the rest. These compotes leave the fruits unpuréed, and rely upon the maceration of fruit in alcohol to provide the softened, sauce-like qualities of the compote. These compotes may be served as desserts in themselves, with the addition of cream or ice-cream to offset the richness of flavour. Alternatively, a few brandied cherries (or any of the other fruit compotes that follow) make a luxurious accompaniment to a creamy dessert.

So take your choice from amongst the twenty-five sauces that you will find in this chapter – and don't forget, variety is your option, since many of the sauces that follow can be altered by the substitution of different fruit of a similar type. If you prefer apricots to plums, pears to apples, blueberries to blackcurrants, then just go ahead!

Coulis d'Amandes

ALMOND SAUCE

Serves 4

Imperial (Metric)	American
8 oz (225g) skinned almonds	*2 cups skinned almonds*
½ pint (300ml) water	*1⅓ cups water*
1 teaspoon cornflour and 5 tablespoons cold water,	*1 teaspoon cornstarch and 5 tablespoons cold water,*
to thicken	*to thicken*
2 fl oz (60ml) natural yogurt	*¼ cup plain yogurt*
Juice of 1 lemon	*Juice of 1 lemon*
1 tablespoon puréed onion or garlic	*1 tablespoon puréed onion or garlic*
or 2 oz (50g) pale honey	*or 4 tablespoons clear honey*

1 Blend the almonds and water to a smooth cream. Place in a pan and bring to the boil. Thicken, if wished, with the cornflour mixture, then stir in the yogurt.

2 Add the lemon juice and then either the savoury or sweet flavouring, according to the use of the sauce. Heat through and serve.

Opposite *Plum and Apple Roll with Armagnac (page 116).*
Overleaf *Pomegranate Blush (page 148) and Peaches Macerated in Beaujolais (page 141).*

Coulis de Pommes zux Müres

APPLE AND BLACKBERRY SAUCE

Serves 4

Imperial (Metric)	American
8 oz (225g) apples	*8 ounces apples*
4 oz (100g) raw cane sugar	*2/3 cup raw cane sugar*
1/2 pint (300ml) dry cider	*1 1/3 cups dry cider*
Small stick cinnamon	*Small stick cinnamon*
1 teaspoon potato starch or cornflour and	*1 teaspoon potato starch or cornstarch and*
5 tablespoons cold cider, to thicken	*5 tablespoons cold cider, to thicken*
8 oz (225g) blackberries	*2 cups blackberries*

1 Peel, core and quarter the apples. Place in a pan with the sugar, cider and cinnamon. Cook until the apples are tender, then strain off the juice. Reserve the apples, discard the cinnamon, and return the juice to the pan.
2 Reheat the juice with the starch slurry and boil for 4 minutes.
3 Return the apples to the pan, add the cleaned berries, and poach for 4 minutes before serving.

Coulis aux Pommes et de Cidre

APPLE-CIDER SAUCE

Serves 4

Imperial (Metric)	American
8 oz (225g) apples	*8 ounces apples*
3 fl oz (90ml) sweet cider	*1/3 cup sweet cider*
Pinch grated nutmeg	*Pinch grated nutmeg*

1 Peel, core and thinly slice the apples. Place in a pan with the cider and nutmeg and simmer until very tender.
2 Purée the sauce and reheat, or leave to cool and serve cold. If wished, the sauce may be thickened with a slurry of starch and water. If crab apples are available, this sauce is extra-special when they are substituted for half the apples.

Coulis d'Abricots

APRICOT SAUCE

Serves 4

Imperial (Metric)	American
8 oz (225g) dried apricots	2 cups dried apricots
½ pint (300ml) sweet vermouth	1⅓ cups sweet vermouth
Cornflour and water, to thicken	Cornstarch and water, to thicken
¼ teaspoon ground cinnamon	¼ teaspoon ground cinnamon
Juice of 1 lemon or 2 tablespoons sherry vinegar	Juice of 1 lemon or 2 tablespoons sherry vinegar
Good pinch cayenne pepper or 1 oz (25g) clear honey	Good pinch cayenne pepper or 2 tablespoons clear honey

1 Soak the fruit overnight in the vermouth. Place in a blender and liquidize to a purée.
2 Transfer the purée to a pan and heat until boiling. Thicken, if wished, with the cornflour slurry and boil for 4 minutes.
3 Depending on whether the sauce is to be savoury or sweet, correct the flavour with cayenne and vinegar or lemon juice and honey. Simmer until of the desired consistency and serve hot or cold.

Coulis d'Avocat

SAUCE OF AVOCADO PURÉE

Serves 4

Imperial (Metric)	American
½ ripe avocado	½ ripe avocado
Juice of 1 lemon	Juice of 1 lemon
2 oz (50g) fresh tomato pulp	⅓ cup fresh tomato pulp
1 clove garlic, crushed	1 clove garlic, crushed
1 tablespoon chopped shallot	1 tablespoon chopped shallot
Pinch sea salt	Pinch sea salt
Pinch chilli pepper	Pinch chili pepper
1 tablespoon chopped tomato	1 tablespoon chopped tomato

1 Place all the ingredients except the chopped tomato into a blender and blend to a smooth purée.
2 Transfer the mixture to a pan and heat through. Just before serving, stir in the chopped tomato for textural and visual appeal.

Coulis de Bananes aux Raisins
BANANA AND RAISIN BUTTER SAUCE

Serves 4

Imperial (Metric)	American
2 oz (50g) melted butter	*¼ cup melted butter*
8 oz (225g) chopped banana	*2 cups chopped banana*
2 fl oz (60ml) clear honey	*4 tablespoons clear honey*
Juice of 1 lime	*Juice of 1 lime*
Cornflour and water, to thicken	*Cornstarch and water, to thicken*
2 oz (50g) seedless raisins	*⅓ cup seedless raisins*
2 tablespoons rum (optional)	*2 tablespoons rum (optional)*

1 Heat the melted butter and fry the banana for 1 minute. Add the honey and cook for a further 3 minutes until the mixture is like butterscotch in consistency.
2 Place the banana mixture and lime juice in a blender and blend to a smooth purée.
3 Place the mixture in a pan and heat through. Add a slurry of cornflour if the mixture is not thick enough for your purpose, and simmer for 4 minutes. Stir in the raisins, and rum if liked. Simmer for a further 3 minutes, then serve.

Coulis de Cassis aux Pommes

BLACKCURRANT AND APPLE SAUCE

Serves 4

Imperial (Metric)	American
4 oz (100g) cleaned blackcurrants	*⅔ cup cleaned blackcurrants*
4 oz (100g) sliced apple	*⅔ cup sliced apple*
2 tablespoons ruby Port	*2 tablespoons ruby Port*
Juice of 1 lemon	*Juice of 1 lemon*
2 tablespoons clear honey	*2 tablespoons clear honey*
Pinch ground gloves	*Pinch ground cloves*

1 Simmer the fruit in the Port and lemon juice for 6 minutes. Sweeten with honey and flavour with ground cloves to taste.
2 Liquidize if wished, and return to the pan to simmer. If necessary, the mixture may be thickened (whether puréed or not) with a slurry of cornflour, in which case, simmer for a further 4 minutes to clear the starch. Serve when simmering.

Coulis de Cerises Jubilé

CHERRIES JUBILEE

Serves 4

Imperial (Metric)	American
½ pint (300ml) red wine	*1⅓ cups red wine*
3 oz (75g) honey	*¼ cup honey*
¼ teaspoon mixed spice	*¼ teaspoon mixed spice*
Cornflour and water, to thicken	*Cornstarch and water, to thicken*
8 oz (225g) black and red cherries	*2 cups black and red cherries*
1 tablespoon Kirsch	*1 tablespoon Kirsch*

1 Boil together the wine, honey and spices. Thicken with starch and boil for 4 minutes to clarify.
2 Halve and pit the cherries, then add to the sauce. Simmer for 6 minutes to soften the fruit.
3 Stir in the Kirsch, cool and serve.

Coulis d'Airelles au Porto

CRANBERRY SAUCE WITH PORT

Serves 4

Imperial (Metric)	*American*
8 oz (225g) cleaned cranberries	*1⅓ cups cleaned cranberries*
½ pint (300ml) ruby Port	*1⅓ cups ruby Port*
1 cinnamon stick	*1 cinnamon stick*
Juice of 1 lemon	*Juice of 1 lemon*
Cornflour and water, to thicken	*Cornstarch and water, to thicken*

1 Simmer the berries in the Port with the stick of cinnamon until the berries are soft. Remove the cinnamon and flavour with lemon juice.
2 Thicken the sauce with starch and boil for 4 minutes to clarify. Leave to cool before serving.

Coulis de Groseilles Vertes

A GREEN GOOSEBERRY SAUCE

Serves 4

Imperial (Metric)	*American*
8 oz (225g) trimmed gooseberries	*1⅓ cups trimmed gooseberries*
3 oz (75g) sliced apple	*½ cup sliced apple*
1 oz (25g) sugar	*2 tablespoons sugar*
3 fl oz (90ml) dry white wine	*⅓ cup dry white wine*
6 fresh mint leaves	*6 fresh mint leaves*
Cornflour and water, to thicken	*Cornstarch and water, to thicken*

1 Place the fruit in a pan with the sugar and wine. Bring to the boil and simmer until tender. Pass the mixture through a strainer – this removes the bitter seeds more effectively. Liquidize the mixture with the mint leaves.
2 Return the mixture to the pan and thicken with starch. Boil for 4 minutes to clarify the sauce. Serve hot or cold. This sauce is also very good with peeled kiwi fruit replacing the gooseberries.

Coulis de Raisins Verts

WHITE GRAPE SAUCE

Serves 4

Imperial (Metric)	*American*
8 oz (225g) skinned seedless grapes (green and unripe)	*2 cups skinned seedless grapes (green and unripe)*
3 oz (75g) sugar	*½ cup sugar*
1 fl oz (30ml) dry white wine	*2 tablespoons dry white wine*
Cornflour and water, to thicken	*Cornstarch and water, to thicken*

1 Poach the grapes in the sugar and wine until the fruit is soft. Purée in a blender.
2 Return the mixture to the pan, stir in the starch and boil for 4 minutes to clear the sauce. Serve hot or cold, with a garnish of seedless grapes which could, if wished, be simmered for a few minutes in the sauce.

Coulis de Mangues au Gingembre

MANGO SAUCE WITH GINGER

Serves 4

Imperial (Metric)	*American*
12 oz (350g) diced ripe mango flesh	*2 cups diced ripe mango flesh*
1 tablespoon chopped fresh ginger	*1 tablespoon chopped fresh ginger*
4 fl oz (120ml) Sauternes	*½ cup Sauternes*
Cornflour and water, to thicken	*Cornstarch and water, to thicken*

1 Boil two-thirds of the mango with the ginger and wine, until the fruit is soft. Purée in a blender.
2 Return to the pan and, if further thickening is required, add a slurry of starch and boil for 4 minutes to cook through. Add the remaining mango and warm through. A handful of raisins added at this stage will give an added dimension of colour, flavour and texture to the sauce, too.

Coulis de Cantaloup au Porto Blanc

MELON AND PORT SAUCE

Serves 4

Imperial (Metric)	American
8 oz (225g) diced Cantaloupe melon	1½ cups diced Cantaloupe melon
2 tablespoons white Port	2 tablespoons white Port
1 teaspoon ground ginger	1 teaspoon ground ginger
2 tablespoons clear honey	2 tablespoons clear honey
Cornflour and water, to thicken	Cornstarch and water, to thicken

1 Liquidize together all the ingredients except the starch. If a thicker sauce is required, place the purée in a pan and add the thickening. Boil for 4 minutes to stabilize and clear the starch. Leave to cool before serving. This sauce is good with a garnish of wild strawberries.

Coulis de Pêches

PEACH AND BERRY SAUCE

Serves 4

Imperial (Metric)	American
2 ripe peaches	2 ripe peaches
1 oz (25g) redcurrant jelly	2 tablespoons redcurrant jelly
1 oz (25g) fresh raspberries	¼ cup fresh raspberries
1 fl oz (30ml) Kirsch	2 tablespoons Kirsch
1 fl oz (30ml) white Port	2 tablespoons white Port
Cornflour and water, to thicken	Cornstarch and water, to thicken

1 Skin, halve and pit the peaches. Chop roughly and place in a blender.
2 Purée together all the ingredients except the starch mixture. If wished, stabilize the sauce by heating with the starch slurry and boiling for 4 minutes to thicken and cook. Cool before using.

Coulis d'Ananas au Gingembre

PINEAPPLE AND APPLE SAUCE WITH GINGER

Serves 4

Imperial (Metric)	American
4 oz (100g) fresh pineapple	*⅔ cup fresh pineapple*
4 oz (100g) chopped apple	*⅔ cup chopped apple*
1 tablespoon chopped fresh ginger	*1 tablespoon chopped fresh ginger*
1 teaspoon soya sauce	*1 teaspoon soy sauce*
1 crushed clove garlic	*1 crushed clove garlic*
1 teaspoon honey	*1 teaspoon honey*
Sea salt	*Sea salt*
Freshly ground pepper	*Freshly ground pepper*

1 Place all the ingredients except the seasoning into a blender and blend to a purée.
2 Transfer the purée to a pan and heat to a boil. Season to taste and serve.

Coulis de Prunes Rouges ou Noires

PLUM AND RED WINE SAUCE

Serves 4

Imperial (Metric)	American
8 oz (225g) skinned and stoned plums*	*1⅓ cups skinned and pitted plums**
1 oz (25g) sugar	*2 tablespoons sugar*
3 fl oz (75ml) red wine	*⅓ cup red wine*
1 teaspoon red wine vinegar	*1 teaspoon red wine vinegar*
1 teaspoon soya sauce	*1 teaspoon soy sauce*
1 crushed clove garlic	*1 crushed clove garlic*
1 teaspoon crushed fresh ginger	*1 teaspoon crushed fresh ginger*
Cornflour and water, to thicken	*Cornstarch and water, to thicken*

1 Place the plums in a pan with all the ingredients except the thickener. Bring to the boil and simmer until the fruit is tender.
2 Purée the mixture in a blender, then return to the pan and bring back to the boil. Add the starch and cook for 4 minutes to clear the sauce. Serve hot.
*Black or red plums may be used – either the Victoria or Quetch variety are suitable.

Coulis de Framboises au Vinaigre

RASPBERRY VINEGAR COULIS

Serves 4

Imperial (Metric)	*American*
1 oz (25g) sugar	*2 tablespoons sugar*
1 fl oz (30ml) raspberry vinegar	*2 tablespoons raspberry vinegar*
8 oz (225g) fresh raspberries	*1⅓ cups fresh raspberries*

1 Boil together the sugar and vinegar. Remove from the heat and stir in the cleaned berries.
2 Place in a blender and reduce to a smooth purée. Sieve, if wished, to remove the pips. Raspberry eau de vie could be substituted for the vinegar, if wished. Serve chilled.

Coulis de Groseilles Rouges

REDCURRANT SAUCE

Serves 4

Imperial (Metric)	*American*
1 lb (450g) redcurrants	*1 pound redcurrants*
2 oz (50g) sugar	*⅓ cup sugar*
Cornflour and water, to thicken	*Cornstarch and water, to thicken*
Juice of ½ lemon	*Juice of ½ lemon*

1 Place the cleaned currants in a blender and purée. Pass through a strainer to extract all the juices.
2 Transfer the redcurrants to a pan, stir in the sugar and bring to the boil. Thicken with the starch and boil for 4 minutes to clear the sauce. Stir in lemon juice to taste and serve hot or chilled.

Coulis de Rhubarbe aux Poires

RHUBARB AND PEAR SAUCE

Serves 4

Imperial (Metric)	American
8 oz (225g) red rhubarb	8 ounces red rhubarb
1 large ripe pear	1 large ripe pear
2 tablespoons clear honey	2 tablespoons clear honey
Pinch ground coriander	Pinch ground coriander

1 Trim off any stringy bits from the rhubarb, then chop into chunks.
2 Peel, core and dice the pear.
3 Place the fruit in a pan with the honey and cook very gently until soft. Cool, then purée in a blender, season with coriander and serve.

Coulis de Fraises à l'Orange

STRAWBERRY AND ORANGE SAUCE

Serves 4

Imperial (Metric)	American
8 oz (225g) strawberries	1⅓ cups strawberries
Juice of 1 orange	Juice of 1 orange
Juice of 1 lemon	Juice of 1 lemon
2 oz (50g) honey	4 tablespoons honey

1 Slice the strawberries and marinate in the juices and honey for at least 1 hour.
2 Place in a blender and purée until smooth. Serve chilled.

Coulis de Tomates à l'Aigre-Doux

SWEET-SOUR TOMATO SAUCE

Serves 4

Imperial (Metric)	American
1 lb (450g) beefsteak tomatoes	1 pound beefsteak tomatoes
1 shallot	1 shallot
2 tablespoons chopped red pepper	2 tablespoons chopped red pepper
2 oz (50g) raw cane sugar	1/3 cup raw cane sugar
Pinch sea salt	Pinch sea salt
Pinch cayenne pepper	Pinch cayenne pepper
2 tablespoons raspberry vinegar	2 tablespoons raspberry vinegar
Snipped herbs of choice	Snipped herbs of choice

1 Skin, seed and chop the tomatoes. Reserve the flesh.

2 Chop the shallot, then place in a pan with the pepper and vinegar. Boil for 2 minutes before adding the sugar, salt and cayenne. Add the tomato flesh, then simmer for 4 minutes.

3 Liquidize the sauce in a blender. Serve cold, sprinkled with the herbs of your choice. Basil is especially good. For a Provençal touch, a clove of garlic, liquidized with a tablespoon of olive oil, can be stirred in when the tomatoes are added to the sauce.

Compote de Griottes à la Fine de Charentes

MORELLO CHERRIES PRESERVED IN BRANDY

Serves 4

Imperial (Metric)	American
6 oz (150g) honey	*½ cup honey*
1 vanilla pod	*1 vanilla pod*
Juice of 1 lemon	*Juice of 1 lemon*
1 pint (600ml) Fine de Charentes	*2½ cups Fine de Charentes*
1 lb (450g) ripe Morello cherries	*3 cups ripe Morello cherries*

1 Heat the honey with the vanilla and lemon juice. Let the vanilla brew in the warm syrup for a while before discarding. Stir in the Fine de Charentes (if unavailable, use brandy).
2 Wash and drain the cherries and place in a large jar. Pour the syrup over the cherries and leave to cool completely. Seal the jar and leave to macerate in a dark, cool place for at least 6 weeks before using.

Compote de Figues de Toulouse

FIGS IN FRONTIGNAN WINE WITH RASPBERRIES

Serves 4

Imperial (Metric)	American
8 fresh ripe figs	*8 fresh ripe figs*
½ pint (300ml) Frontignan wine	*1⅓ cups Frontignan wine*
Cornflour and water, to thicken	*Cornstarch and water, to thicken*
6 oz (150g) fresh raspberries	*1 cup fresh raspberries*

1 Wash the figs well, then poach in the wine for 12 minutes. Remove with a slotted spoon and reserve.
2 Thicken the juices by boiling with the starch for 4 minutes. Return the figs to the pan with the raspberries, and heat through. Serve warm or at room temperature. A little honey may be added to the dish if desired.

Compote de Pêches au Beaujolais

PEACHES, MACERATED IN BEAUJOLAIS

Serves 4

Imperial (Metric)	American
4 ripe peaches	4 ripe peaches
2 oranges	2 oranges
1 pint (600ml) Beaujolais	2½ cups Beaujolais
2 sticks cinnamon	2 sticks cinnamon
3 oz (75ml) honey	¼ cup honey

1 Skin, halve and pit the peaches. Slice the oranges into wafer-thin rounds, removing any pips. Place the fruits in a glass punch bowl.
2 Bring the wine to the boil with the cinnamon and honey. Boil for 2 minutes, then pour over the fruit. Leave to macerate for at least 24 hours. Tiny strawberries may be added when the wine is cold, to macerate along with the peaches and oranges.

Illustrated opposite page 129.

Compote de Pruneaux d'Agen au Thé

BRANDIED PRUNE COMPOTE

Serves 4

Imperial (Metric)	*American*
½ pint (300ml) boiling water	1⅓ cups boiling water
2 Ceylon tea bags	2 Ceylon tea bags
½ lb (225g) prunes	8 ounces prunes
Cornflour and water, to thicken	Cornstarch and water, to thicken
4 oz (100g) dark honey	⅓ cup dark honey
2 fl oz (60ml) brandy	¼ cup brandy

1 Pour boiling water over the tea bags and leave to brew, covered, for 6 minutes. Remove the tea bags, then soak the prunes overnight in the liquid.

2 Next day, stew the prunes gently in the soaking liquid for 12 minutes. Remove the prunes with a slotted spoon and reserve.

3 Stir the slurry of starch into the juices, bring to the boil and cook for 4 minutes to clear the starch and thicken the liquid.

4 Return the prunes to the pan, stir in the honey and brandy and warm through. Serve warm or at room temperature, with thick cream.

CHAPTER NINE

Les Boissons Rafraichissantes

Refreshing, Fruited Drinks

For this final chapter, we have assembled a collection of twenty recipes that need no cooking at all, because they rely upon just the simple amalgam of fruits or fruit juices, dairy produce, water or – on the case of the latter ten recipes – alcohol. Fruit has always been at the heart of humanity's drinking preferences, after good pure water itself, of course. From the simple satisfaction of halving and squeezing a ripe orange, or preparing a jug of refreshing home-made lemonade on a hot Summer's day, to the skills of the winemakers and distillers, that have been with us since the dawn of time, the produce of the bushes, trees and vines has been an inspiration and a satisfaction to the developing palate.

In France, the use of fruit in wines, spirits and liqueurs is perhaps second to none. The Romans planted our earliest vineyards, and the monks created many of our finest liqueurs. Our wines and spirits have, however, been adopted by connoisseurs and simple folk alike around the world as the very pinnacle of French produce and the indispensable accompaniment to a good meal.

The scope of this chapter is too brief to allow a foray into the art of country wine-making – that is at least one book in itself. So we must confine ourselves here to a delicious selection of rather special fruited drinks. First, ten appetizing combinations of good, natural ingredients that can be enjoyed at any time of day – perfect for breakfast, for drivers, for young people, or simply for those who like to keep a clear head whilst enjoying a satisfying, flavoursome and healthy drink. Then, ten exceptional fruity cocktails for that special occasion. In the tradition of that classic French aperitif, Kir, which combines white Burgundy with a splash of blackcurrant-based Cassis liqueur, the marrying of fruit flavours with the heady delights of wines or spirits is well worth trying out and developing further.

So prepare plenty of ice, take one sunny day or Summer evening, add a dash of good company, put the car keys away – and get blending!

143

L'Ananade

PINEAPPLE FIZZ

Serves 4

Imperial (Metric)	American
8 oz (225g) diced fresh pineapple	*1½ cups diced fresh pineapple*
2 oz (50g) honey	*4 tablespoons honey*
4 fl oz (120ml) water	*½ cup water*
2 egg whites	*2 egg whites*
1½ pints (750ml) soda water	*3¾ cups soda water*
Extra pineapple slices, to garnish	*Extra pineapple slices, to garnish*

1 Place the diced pineapple, honey, water and egg whites in a blender, and process to a purée. Strain through muslin into a jug, pushing through all the juices to leave only the pulp behind.
2 Pour the pineapple juice into 4 tall glasses filled with a little crushed ice, and top up with chilled soda water. Decorate with sliced pineapple and serve at once.

Lait de Coco à l'Ananas

COCONUT-PINEAPPLE CREAM

Serves 4

Imperial (Metric)	American
1 pint (600ml) coconut milk	*2½ cups coconut milk*
10 oz (300g) diced fresh pineapple	*2 cups diced fresh pineapple*
2 teaspoons honey	*2 teaspoons honey*
4 slices orange	*4 slices orange*

1 Place the coconut milk, pineapple and honey in a blender and whizz at high speed for 2 minutes.
2 Place some crushed ice in 4 stumpy tumblers and fill with the drink. Float a slice of orange on each and serve at once.

Lait de Coco à la Papaye

PAWPAW (PAPAYA) AND COCONUT SMOOTHIE

Serves 2

Imperial (Metric)	*American*
1 ripe pawpaw, peeled, seeded and chopped	*1 ripe papaya, peeled, pitted and chopped*
Juice of 1 lime	*Juice of 1 lime*
2 teaspoons honey	*2 teaspoons honey*
½ pint (300ml) coconut milk	*1⅓ cups coconut milk*
Sliced lime, to garnish	*Sliced lime, to garnish*

1 Place all the ingredients in a blender and whizz at high speed for a minute.
2 Strain through a muslin cloth into a jug. Fill 2 tall glasses with crushed ice and slices of lime, then pour the drink over. Serve at once.

La Mangoade

MANGO FROTH

Serves 4

Imperial (Metric)	*American*
2 ripe mangoes	*2 ripe mangoes*
2 oz (50g) grated carrot	*⅓ cup grated carrot*
2 oz (50g) honey	*4 tablespoons honey*
¾ pint (425ml) orange juice	*2 cups orange juice*
¼ pint (150ml) hot water	*⅔ cup hot water*
¼ pint (150ml) lemon juice	*⅔ cup lemon juice*
2 egg whites	*2 egg whites*

1 Place all the ingredients in a blender and liquidize to a smooth purée. Pass through a muslin cloth into a jug half-filled with crushed ice. Serve, garnished with sprigs of mint.

Banane à l'Orange

BANANA-ORANGE COOLER

Serves 2

Imperial (Metric)	American
2 ripe bananas, peeled and chopped	2 ripe bananas, peeled and chopped
¼ pint (150ml) orange juice	⅔ cup orange juice
¼ pint (150ml) natural yogurt	⅔ cup plain yogurt
1 tablespoon honey	1 tablespoon honey
Pinch grated nutmeg	Pinch grated nutmeg

1 Place all the ingredients in a blender and purée to a smooth cream. Serve in cocktail glasses with a little extra nutmeg sprinkled on top.

Pamplemousse à la Menthe

MINTED GRAPEFRUIT SHERBET

Serves 2

Imperial (Metric)	American
¾ pint (425ml) grapefruit juice	2 cups grapefruit juice
2 oz (50g) honey	4 tablespoons honey
4 chopped mint leaves	4 chopped mint leaves
Juice of 1 lemon	Juice of 1 lemon
2 teaspoons green mint syrup	2 teaspoons green mint syrup
2 egg whites	2 egg whites

1 Place all the ingredients in a blender and blend to a light froth. Place a little crushed ice in the base of 2 tall champagne flutes and spoon a teaspoon of green mint syrup (or crème de menthe, if preferred) over each, then carefully fill with the drink. Serve at once.

Groseille de la Nouvelle Zéalande

KIWI SPECIAL

Serves 2

Imperial (Metric)	American
6 large kiwi fruit	6 large kiwi fruit
½ pint (300ml) water	1⅓ cups water
3 oz (75g) honey	¼ cup honey
¼ pint (150ml) natural yogurt	⅔ cup plain yogurt

1 Peel the kiwi fruit. Cut 2 thin slices from the centre of 1 fruit, then chop all the remaining flesh into chunks.
2 Place the chopped fruit in a pan with the water and honey. Simmer gently for 6 minutes, then allow to cool before puréeing with the yogurt.
3 Place some crushed ice in 2 cocktail glasses and pour in the drink. Float a slice of kiwi fruit on the surface of each, then serve at once.

La Grenadine

POMEGRANATE BLUSH

Serves 2

Imperial (Metric)	**American**
4 ripe pomegranates	*4 ripe pomegranates*
Juice of 2 blood oranges	*Juice of 2 ruby red oranges*
4 oz (100g) pine nuts	*⅔ cup pine nuts*
2 tablespoons honey	*2 tablespoons honey*
4 tablespoons natural yogurt	*4 tablespoons plain yogurt*
Orange slices, to garnish	*Orange slices, to garnish*

1 Halve the pomegranates. Reserve 2 tablespoons of whole, fruited seeds and pass the rest of the flesh through a fine strainer to extract the juice and leave the black seeds behind.
2 Place the pine nuts in a blender with a little of the orange juice and the honey, and blend to a thin cream.
3 Swirl together the pomegranate juice, nut cream, the remaining orange juice and the yogurt in a jug.
4 Half-fill 2 tall glasses with crushed ice, then fill with the drink. Garnish with slices of pink-flecked orange and serve at once.
Illustrated opposite page 129.

Melonade aux Framboises

MELON AND RASPBERRY SPARKLE

Serves 4

Imperial (Metric)	**American**
Flesh from 1 large Ogen melon	*Flesh from 1 large Ogen melon*
2 egg whites	*2 egg whites*
6 skinned almonds	*6 skinned almonds*
6 oz (150g) fresh raspberries	*1 cup fresh raspberries*
3 tablespoons honey	*3 tablespoons honey*
4 fl oz (120ml) natural yogurt	*½ cup plain yogurt*
Soda water, to serve	*Soda water, to serve*
Extra raspberries, to garnish	*Extra raspberries, to garnish*

1 Place all but the last two ingredients into a blender and whizz to a creamy froth. Strain, if wished, to remove the raspberry seeds, but this is not necessary.
2 Pour over crushed ice into 4 tall tumblers. Top up with a squirt of soda and decorate with berries before serving.

La Plaquemine

PERSIMMON DREAM

Serves 4

Imperial (Metric)	American
4 large, ripe persimmons	*4 large, ripe persimmons*
Juice of 2 lemons	*Juice of 2 lemons*
2 egg whites	*2 egg whites*
Pinch sea salt	*Pinch sea salt*
3 tablespoons honey	*3 tablespoons honey*
3 fl oz (90ml) buttermilk	*⅓ cup buttermilk*
Borage flowers, to garnish	*Borage flowers, to garnish*

1 Peel the persimmons and remove the stones. Chop the flesh roughly.
2 Place all the ingredients except the garnish into a blender. Process until smooth. Half fill a jug with crushed ice and pour in the drink. Float borage flowers on the top before pouring into chunky tumblers.

Coupe de la Forêt

BERRY AND CHABLIS CUP

Serves 4

Imperial (Metric)	*American*
6 oz (150g) mixed berries of choice	*1 cup mixed berries of choice*
1 fl oz (30ml) Cointreau	*2 tablespoons Cointreau*
1 fl oz (30ml) brandy	*2 tablespoons brandy*
1 bottle Chablis	*1 bottle Chablis*
2 slices lemon	*2 slices lemon*
2 slices orange	*2 slices orange*
2 slices cucumber	*2 slices cucumber*
Sprigs borage	*Sprigs borage*

1 Place the berries in a punch bowl and swirl with the spirits. Leave to macerate for 30 minutes.
2 Pour on the chilled Chablis, then float the remaining ingredients on the surface, along with a few ice cubes. Serve at once.

Kaltschale d'Ananas

PINEAPPLE HOCK

Serves 4

Imperial (Metric)	*American*
1 pineapple	*1 pineapple*
Juice of 1 lemon	*Juice of 1 lemon*
Juice of 2 oranges	*Juice of 2 oranges*
2 fl oz (60ml) Kirsch	*¼ cup Kirsch*
1 bottle good hock	*1 bottle good Hock*

1 Peel the pineapple and cut into very small pieces. Mix in a jug with the juices and Kirsch. Leave to macerate for 30 minutes.
2 Top up with chilled Hock and add a few ice cubes. Serve at once.

Cassis Mousseux

BLACKCURRANT CHAMPAGNE FIZZ

Serves 1

Imperial (Metric)	*American*
1 egg white	*1 egg white*
Juice of ½ lemon	*Juice of ½ lemon*
4 tablespoons gin	*4 tablespoons gin*
2 tablespoons Crème de Cassis	*2 tablespoons Crème de Cassis*
¼ bottle Champagne	*¼ bottle Champagne*
Sprig fresh blackcurrants	*Sprig fresh blackcurrants*

1 Place the egg white, lemon, gin and Cassis in a cocktail shaker or chilled glass jar with 2 tablespoons crushed ice. Shake until well mixed.

2 Strain the mixture into a large champagne flute and top up with Champagne. Decorate with a sprig of berries and serve.

La Coupe Normande

NORMANDY PUNCH

Serves 4

Imperial (Metric)	*American*
1 ripe apple	*1 ripe apple*
1 fl oz (30ml) Calvados	*2 tablespoons Calvados*
Juice of 1 lemon	*Juice of 1 lemon*
Piece of cucumber peel	*Piece of cucumber peel*
1 bottle Normandy cider	*1 bottle Normandy cider*

1 Core and thinly slice the apple. Place in an earthenware jug with the Calvados, lemon juice and cucumber peel. Leave to macerate for 15 minutes.

2 Pour in a bottle of chilled cider, add a few ice cubes and serve.

Coupe Maritime

NAVY CUP

Serves 4

Imperial (Metric)	*American*
8 fl oz (250ml) rum	*1 cup rum*
4 oz (100g) Maraschino cherries	*⅔ cup Maraschino cherries*
Juice of 2 lemons	*Juice of 2 lemons*
1 bottle Champagne	*1 bottle Champagne*

1 Place the rum, cherries and lemon juice in a punch bowl and pour on the chilled champagne. Add a few ice cubes and serve at once.

Tahiti à la Gauguin

EXOTIC COCKTAIL

Serves 1

Imperial (Metric)	*American*
1 tablespoon vodka	*1 tablespoon vodka*
1 tablespoon white rum	*1 tablespoon white rum*
Juice of 2 lemons	*Juice of 2 lemons*
2 egg whites	*2 egg whites*
¼ pint (150ml) mixed fruit juice	*⅔ cup mixed juice*
1 tablespoon blue Curaçao	*1 tablespoon blue Curaçao*

1 Place all the ingredients in a blender with 2 ice cubes and whizz to a froth.
2 Pour into a tall glass and decorate with an exotic flower.

L'Ananas Tropicale

TIPSY PINEAPPLE

Serves 1

Imperial (Metric)	*American*
1 whole pineapple	*1 whole pineapple*
3 tablespoons dark rum	*3 tablespoons dark rum*
3 fl oz (90ml) dry vermouth	*⅓ cup dry vermouth*
2 sprigs fresh mint	*2 sprigs fresh mint*

1 Cut the top off the pineapple and scoop out as much of the flesh as you can, discarding the fibrous centre.

2 Place the fruit in a blender with the rum, vermouth and mint. Blend to a purée with crushed ice.

3 Pour the drink into the scooped-out pineapple shell. Cover the pineapple with its 'hat', tilted to leave space for a straw. Serve.

Le Délice d'Abricot

APRICOT NECTAR

Serves 1

Imperial (Metric)	*American*
2 ripe apricots	*2 ripe apricots*
2 tablespoons Marc de Bourgogne	*2 tablespoons Marc de Bourgogne*
Juice of 1 lemon	*Juice of 1 lemon*
Soda water	*Soda water*
Toasted grated coconut to garnish	*Toasted grated coconut to garnish*

1 Skin and stone the apricots. Chop roughly and place in a blender with the Marc, lemon juice and 2 ice cubes. Blend to a smooth purée.

2 Pour the apricot purée into a tall cocktail glass, top up with soda water and sprinkle with coconut before serving.

La Mangue de la Jamaique

JAMAICAN MANGO REFRESHER

Serves 2

Imperial (Metric)	**American**
4 ripe mangoes	4 ripe mangoes
Juice of 4 limes	Juice of 4 limes
Juice of 2 oranges	Juice of 2 oranges
4 fl oz (120ml) dry vermouth	½ cup dry vermouth
¼ pint iced water	⅔ cup iced water
1 teaspoon preserved ginger	1 teaspoon preserved ginger
1 tablespoon ginger syrup	1 tablespoon ginger syrup

1 Peel and pit the mangoes, and dice the flesh. Place in a blender with all the other ingredients and blend to a smooth purée.

2 Pour the drink into a tall jug, add crushed ice and decorate with twists of lime peel. Serve.

Bellini Tropicale
TROPICAL FIZZ

Serves 4

Imperial (Metric)	*American*
Juice of 3 tangerines	*Juice of 3 tangerines*
Juice of 3 limes	*Juice of 3 limes*
Pulp of 3 passion fruit	*Pulp of 3 passion fruit*
1 slice pineapple, chopped	*1 slice pineapple, chopped*
Grated rind of ½ lime	*Grated rind of ½ lime*
6 oz (150g) raw cane sugar	*1 cup raw cane sugar*
1 small bottle dry ginger ale	*1 small bottle Canada Dry*
1 bottle Champagne	*1 bottle Champagne*
1 paw paw, scooped into balls	*1 papaya, scooped into balls*

1 Place the fruit juices, passion fruit pulp, pineapple and grated rind in a pan with the sugar. Heat gently, until the sugar has dissolved. Remove from the heat and allow to cool.
2 Pour the fruit mixture into a tall jug and pour on the ginger ale and Champagne. Stir in the paw paw balls and serve.

Index